AMERICA'S VICTIMS

*Opposing
Viewpoints®*

Other Books of Related Interest

Opposing Viewpoints Series

American Values
Child Abuse
Civil Liberties
Criminal Justice
The Homeless
Immigration
The Legal System
Mental Illness
Politics in America
Poverty
Race Relations
Social Justice
Violence in America

Current Controversies Series

Ethics
Family Violence
Hate Crimes
Illegal Immigration
Sexual Harassment
Violence Against Women

At Issues Series

Affirmative Action
Domestic Violence
Environmental Justice
Ethnic Conflict
Immigration Policy
Rape on Campus

AMERICA'S VICTIMS

Opposing Viewpoints®

David Bender & Bruno Leone, *Series Editors*

Paul A. Winters, *Book Editor*

OPPOSING
VIEWPOINTS®
SERIES

Greenhaven Press, Inc., San Diego, CA

Cover photo: Wayzata Technology

Greenhaven Press, Inc.
PO Box 289009
San Diego, CA 92198-9009

Library of Congress Cataloging-in-Publication Data

America's victims : opposing viewpoints / Paul A. Winters, book
  editor.
        p.   cm. — (Opposing viewpoints series)
    Includes bibliographical references and index.
    ISBN 1-56510-401-3 (lib. : alk. paper). — ISBN 1-56510-400-5
(pbk. : alk. paper)
        1. Entitlement attitudes—Social aspects—United States.
2. Victims—United States. 3. Blame—Moral and ethical aspects.
4. Justice—United States. 5. Civil rights—United States.
6. United States—Moral conditions. 7. United States—Social
policy—1993- . 8. United States—Social conditions—1945- .
I. Winters, Paul A., 1965- . II. Series: Opposing viewpoints
series (Unnumbered)
HN90.M6A47   1996
306'.9073—dc20   95-49648
                                                                       CIP

Every effort has been made to trace the owners of copyrighted material.

"Congress shall make no law . . . abridging the freedom of speech, or of the press."

First Amendment to the U.S. Constitution

The basic foundation of our democracy is the First Amendment guarantee of freedom of expression. The Opposing Viewpoints Series is dedicated to the concept of this basic freedom and the idea that it is more important to practice it than to enshrine it.

Contents

Why Consider Opposing Viewpoints?

"The only way in which a human being can make some approach to knowing the whole of a subject is by hearing what can be said about it by persons of every variety of opinion and studying all modes in which it can be looked at by every character of mind. No wise man ever acquired his wisdom in any mode but this."

John Stuart Mill

In our media-intensive culture it is not difficult to find differing opinions. Thousands of newspapers and magazines and dozens of radio and television talk shows resound with differing points of view. The difficulty lies in deciding which opinion to agree with and which "experts" seem the most credible. The more inundated we become with differing opinions and claims, the more essential it is to hone critical reading and thinking skills to evaluate these ideas. Opposing Viewpoints books address this problem directly by presenting stimulating debates that can be used to enhance and teach these skills. The varied opinions contained in each book examine many different aspects of a single issue. While examining these conveniently edited opposing views, readers can develop critical thinking skills such as the ability to compare and contrast authors' credibility, facts, argumentation styles, use of persuasive techniques, and other stylistic tools. In short, the Opposing Viewpoints Series is an ideal way to attain the higher-level thinking and reading skills so essential in a culture of diverse and contradictory opinions.

In addition to providing a tool for critical thinking, Opposing Viewpoints books challenge readers to question their own strongly held opinions and assumptions. Most people form their opinions on the basis of upbringing, peer pressure, and personal, cultural, or professional bias. By reading carefully balanced opposing views, readers must directly confront new ideas as well as the opinions of those with whom they disagree. This is not to simplistically argue that everyone who reads opposing views will—or should—change his or her opinion. Instead, the series enhances readers' depth of understanding of their own views by encouraging confrontation with opposing ideas. Careful examination of others' views can lead to the readers' understanding of the logical inconsistencies in their own opinions, perspective on why they hold an opinion, and the consideration of the possibility that their opinion requires further evaluation.

Evaluating Other Opinions

To ensure that this type of examination occurs, Opposing Viewpoints books present all types of opinions. Prominent spokespeople on different sides of each issue as well as well-known professionals from many disciplines challenge the reader. An additional goal of the series is to provide a forum for other, less known, or even unpopular viewpoints. The opinion of an ordinary person who has had to make the decision to cut off life support from a terminally ill relative, for example, may be just as valuable and provide just as much insight as a medical ethicist's professional opinion. The editors have two additional purposes in including these less known views. One, the editors encourage readers to respect others' opinions—even when not enhanced by professional credibility. It is only by reading or listening to and objectively evaluating others' ideas that one can determine whether they are worthy of consideration. Two, the inclusion of such viewpoints encourages the important critical thinking skill of objectively evaluating an author's credentials and bias. This evaluation will illuminate an author's reasons for taking a particular stance on an issue and will aid in readers' evaluation of the author's ideas.

As series editors of the Opposing Viewpoints Series, it is our hope that these books will give readers a deeper understanding of the issues debated and an appreciation of the complexity of even seemingly simple issues when good and honest people disagree. This awareness is particularly important in a democratic society such as ours in which people enter into public debate to determine the common good. Those with whom one disagrees should not be regarded as enemies but rather as people whose views deserve careful examination and may shed light on one's own.

Thomas Jefferson once said that "difference of opinion leads to inquiry, and inquiry to truth." Jefferson, a broadly educated man, argued that "if a nation expects to be ignorant and free . . . it expects what never was and never will be." As individuals and as a nation, it is imperative that we consider the opinions of others and examine them with skill and discernment. The Opposing Viewpoints Series is intended to help readers achieve this goal.

David L. Bender & Bruno Leone,
Series Editors

Introduction

"American life is increasingly characterized by the plaintive insistence, I am a victim.*"*

Charles J. Sykes

A number of observers of American society in the 1990s have bemoaned what *A Nation of Victims* author Charles J. Sykes calls "the decay of the American character." Sykes deplores the growing tendency of self-designated victims to abdicate personal responsibility for their problems. "The new culture," he states, "reflects a readiness not merely to feel sorry for oneself but to wield one's resentments as weapons of social advantage and to regard deficiencies as entitlements to society's deference." Other social observers, however, counter that such arguments stem from a backlash against the political success of the feminist and civil rights movements since the 1960s. Robert Hughes, a senior writer for *Time* magazine and the author of *Culture of Complaint: The Fraying of America*, argues that conservatives are using rhetoric about personal responsibility to erode broad societal support for feminist and civil rights agendas. On one side of the debate are those like Sykes who denounce the decay of personal responsibility in American culture, while on the other are those such as Hughes who lament the undermining of social responsibility.

Sykes is one of the most ardent critics decrying the detrimental effects that increasing claims of victimhood have on American society. "A community of interdependent citizens," he asserts, "has been displaced by a society of resentful, competing, and self-interested individuals who have dressed their private annoyances in the garb of victimism." In this new culture, Sykes argues, moral authority and political advantage are gained through claims of past (or continued) injustice. As a result, he contends, society is breaking down into self-described victim groups—"women, blacks, youths, Native Americans, the unemployed, the poor"—who compete for the status of most oppressed. According to Sykes, these groups use their moral authority as victims to make demands for political, social, and economic advantages that they claim are necessary to redress past inequality. But, Sykes argues, these demands test the limits of society's generosity. Americans have always been compassionate toward the less fortunate, he maintains, "but our concern for the genuine victims of misfortune or injustice is sorely tested as the list of certifiable victims continues to grow." As the numbers of self-defined victims increases, social concern among other Americans decreases, Sykes concludes.

Other social commentators dispute Sykes's view, claiming that such arguments undermine the success of rights movements that have gained needed economic and legal protections for disadvantaged groups such as women, minorities, and the poor. Feminist author and antipornography activist Andrea Dworkin argues that since the 1960s these movements have made great strides toward changing oppressive attitudes toward women and minorities and drawing such previously oppressed groups fully into the mainstream of American society, economy, and culture. "The civil rights movement showed the world that the concept of human dignity is not an abstract idea," she asserts. Many social commentators contend, however, that during the 1980s and 1990s a political backlash increased resistance to the women's and civil rights movements. Opponents successfully characterized the rights movements as shrill and excessive in their demands, these commentators maintain. As a result, according to Dworkin, women and minorities feel that there is no longer "a chance for those who have been hurt to say the ways in which they have been hurt and to try to get the society to redress the grievance." The various rights movements, she maintains, must continue to demand that the rest of society meet standards of equality and justice and community.

However, an increasing number of people who support the goals of political and economic inclusion that the civil rights and women's liberation movements seek agree in part with Sykes's argument. They concede that the movements have gone too far in the direction of individual interests and that their excesses have undermined Americans' sense of community and moral responsibility. Elizabeth Fox-Genovese, author of *Feminism Without Illusions: A Critique of Individualism*, argues that among the excesses were the movements' efforts to overturn the traditional morality of American culture, which they saw as "oppressive" and "hypocritical." Among the unanticipated results of disparaging traditional morality, according to Fox-Genovese, was the erosion of Americans' traditional sense of economic fair play and compassion for the underdog. By attacking Americans' morality, she argues, these groups undermined social support for movements that advocated economic opportunities for the disadvantaged. "Economic issues are moral issues," she maintains: The redistribution of economic and political advantages requires a moral consensus within the society. Fox-Genovese faults liberation movements for failing to admit that they are seeking to impose new standards of morality upon

13

society and, more importantly, for failing to develop a broad community consensus on the new standards. As a result of these failures, she contends, the goals of the movements and of the political left in general have been discredited. Fox-Genovese and other civil rights supporters have called for a moral reawakening in American society and a new consensus on issues of social concern.

The debate over "victimhood" has extended into many areas of American life other than the civil rights movement, from criminal and civil law to psychology. *America's Victims: Opposing Viewpoints* explores the effects of victimhood on American society in the following chapters: How Is "Victimhood" Affecting American Society? Has the Civil Rights Movement Become a "Victimhood" Competition? Does the Recovery Movement Create Victims? How Does "Victimhood" Affect the American Justice System?

How Is "Victimhood" Affecting American Society?

Chapter Preface

Crybabies and busybodies, characterized by "a nasty intolerance and a desire to blame everyone else for everything," are turning America into "A Nation of Finger Pointers," according to Lance Morrow, senior writer for *Time* magazine. Crybabies, on the one hand, advance claims of victimhood and pursue rights and entitlements they say are necessary to overcome their victim status. Busybodies, on the other hand, seek to ban a lengthening list of "offensive" behaviors that, according to them, violate their right not to be offended. "Victims . . . derive identity, innocence and a kind of devious power from sheer, defaulting helplessness," Morrow asserts. At the same time, "busybodies have begun to infect American society with a nasty intolerance—a zeal to police the private lives of others," he contends.

Time contributor John Elson, among many other social commentators, decries what he calls the neopuritanism in American society exhibited by such phenomena as political correctness on college campuses and antismoking campaigns in corporations and public places. He argues that these campaigns are the result of arbitrary efforts by groups to impose "their own standards of behavior, health and thought" on the rest of society. Elson states, "Busybodies . . . seem to have lost sight of a bedrock American virtue: tolerance, allowing others, in the name of freedom, to do things one disagrees with or does not like, provided they do no outright harm to others."

Elizabeth Fox-Genovese, author of *Feminism Without Illusions: A Critique of Individualism*, is among those who criticize the excessive individualism inherent in Elson's view of tolerance. "Human liberation," she argues, "requires either that no one ever tell anyone else what to do, or that a few impose their specific moral program upon the rest." Fox-Genovese believes that the freedom guaranteed to individuals in American society should be exercised within a framework of moral values established by the community. She states, "An individual is moral only in the measure that he or she conforms to the prevailing standards of a community, which means in the measure that he or she observes some fundamental rules." According to Fox-Genovese, moral standards should be enforced by community members in order to promote social responsibility.

Whether "victims" and "busybodies" have positive or negative effect on American society is a contentious subject. The viewpoints in the following chapter explore this controversy.

16

"Victimism . . . has exacted a heavy tax on our compassion and on the sense of guilt that is so integral a part of the politics of victimization."

Claims of Victimhood Cause Compassion Fatigue

Charles J. Sykes

Many writers have noted a growing divisiveness in American society. In the following viewpoint, Charles J. Sykes asserts that this divisiveness is the result of various groups' insistent claims of an unassailable moral authority based on victimhood and an entitlement to society's sympathy. Competing claims of victimhood, according to Sykes, lead to a lack of compassion for real victims and a decay of Americans' sense of morality and equity. Sykes is the author of *A Nation of Victims: The Decay of the American Character*, from which this viewpoint is excerpted.

As you read, consider the following questions:

1. What does it mean to be sensitive in terms of what Sykes calls "victimspeak"?
2. How does victimism debilitate victims, according to the author?
3. How does the author define "compassion fatigue"?

Something extraordinary is happening in American society. Crisscrossed by invisible trip wires of emotional, racial, sexual, and psychological grievance, American life is increasingly characterized by the plaintive insistence, *I am a victim.*

The victim-ization of America is remarkably egalitarian. From the addicts of the South Bronx to the self-styled emotional road-kills of Manhattan's Upper East Side, the mantra of the victims is the same: *I am not responsible; it's not my fault.*

Paradoxically, this don't-blame-me permissiveness is applied only to the self, not to others; it is compatible with an ideological puritanism that is notable for its shrill demands of psychological, political, and linguistic correctness. The ethos of victimization has an endless capacity not only for exculpating one's self from blame, washing away responsibility in a torrent of explanation—racism, sexism, rotten parents, addiction, and illness—but also for projecting guilt onto others.

If previous movements of liberation may have been characterized as Revolutions of Rising Expectations, this society is in the grips of a Revolution of Rising Sensitivities, in which grievance begets grievance. In the society of victims, individuals compete not only for rights or economic advantage but also for points on the "sensitivity" index, where "feelings" rather than reason are what count. . . .

The Tone of the Current Debate

The claim that we are all victims accounts not only for what one critic calls an outbreak of "emotional influenza" in the United States but also for the increasingly shrill and carping tone of social debate—and for the distrust and unease in our day-to-day relations. At times it seems that we can no longer talk to one another. Or rather, we can talk—and shout, demand, and vilify—but we cannot reason. We lack agreed-upon standards to which we can refer our disputes. In the absence of shared notions of justice or equity, many of the issues we confront appear increasingly to be unresolvable.

For many Americans, the politics of victimization has taken the place of more traditional expressions of morality and equity. "The simple act of naming and identifying victims becomes a substitute for conscience and public discourse," writes Joseph Amato. "Identifying oneself with the 'real suffering' of a chosen class, people, group, race, sex, or historical victim is the communion call of the twentieth-century secular individual. It is his sincerity, his holiness, his martyrdom."

Political discourse and academic research alike have become dominated by what University of Chicago sociologist James Coleman calls the politics of "conspicuous benevolence," which is designed to "display, ostentatiously even, egalitarian intentions." Among his academic colleagues, Coleman gibes, postures of conspicuous benevolence have replaced "the patterns of conspicuous consumption that Thorstein Veblen attributed to the rich. . . . They display, conspicuously, the benevolent intentions of their supporters."

Divisiveness Rather than Pluralism

This attitude may account not only for the paucity of serious public debate but also for growing divisiveness along lines of race, class, and gender, and for the tribalization of American society as groups define themselves not by their individual worth or shared culture but solely by their status as victims. Americans have long prided themselves on their pluralism and their tolerance of the incredible diversity of viewpoints and ideologies represented by this country's various cultural groups. But insistence on the irreducible quality of one's victimhood threatens to turn pluralism into a series of prisons. Only genuine victims can claim "sensitivity" and "authenticity," and only victims can challenge other victims.

Increasingly, debates take place between antagonists who deny their opponents' ability to understand their plight. Inevitably, that turns such clashes into increasingly bitter ad hominem attacks in which victim status and the insistent demands for sensitivity are played as trump cards. In a culture of sound bites and slogans substituted for rational argument, the claim that one is a victim has become one of the few universally recognized currencies of intellectual exchange. Victimspeak is the trigger that permits the unleashing of an emotional and self-righteous response to any perceived slight. Charges of racism and sexism continue to be the nuclear weapons of debate, used to shout down nuanced approaches to complex issues. Victimspeak insists upon moral superiority and moral absolutism and thus tends to put an abrupt end to conversation; the threat of its deployment is usually enough to keep others from even considering raising a controversial subject. Ironically, this style of linguistic bullying often parades under the banner of "sensitivity."

Of course, sensitivity to the needs and concerns of others is the mark of a civil and civilized society. But the victimist demand for sensitivity is more problematic. To be sensitive (in victimspeak) is not to argue or to reason but to *feel*, to attune one's response to another's sense of aggrievement. This politicized sensitivity (as distinct from decency, civility, and honesty) demands the constant adjustment of one's responses to the shifting and unpredictable demands of the victim. The greater the wounds, the louder the cries of injustice, the greater the demand for sensitivity—no matter how unreasonable. Asking the wrong questions can be perceived as insensitivity, but so can

19

failing to ask the right ones. One can be insensitive without intending to be; only the victim can judge. Inevitably, this changes both the terms and the climate of debate. It is no longer necessary to engage in lengthy and detailed debate over such issues as affirmative action; it is far easier and more effective to simply brand a critic as insensitive.

Victim vs. Victim

This tactic tends to work as long as there is a consensus about who is the real victim and who the real oppressor. The hierarchy becomes less clear as victim groups begin to vie *with one another* for the right to define the nature of sensitivity. The dominance of victimspeak in American society was dramatically highlighted during the 1991 battle over the confirmation of Clarence Thomas to the U.S. Supreme Court, when both sides—accuser [Anita Hill] and accused alike—portrayed themselves as victims: one of sexual harassment, the other of racism and a "high-tech lynching."

Increasingly, victim-vs.-victim politics seems to frame our social and political debates. There was a certain poignant inevitability about the headline in the *Wall Street Journal* that declare, "Tales From an Oppressed Class"—the oppressed class in question being white males. But the politics of racial resentment is not really all that different from the politics of racial grievance. White racist David Duke is not the opposite of black racist Louis Farrakhan; he is the mirror image. The same can be said of the relationship between the embryonic "men's rights" movement and the feminist movement—the men's movement is far closer to being a clone than a challenge.

Calvin and Hobbes, © Watterson. Reprinted with permission of Universal Press Syndicate.

Tragically, a victim's rage that is redirected from the oppressor toward rival victim groups ultimately turns against the victim himself. For self-hatred is the final destination of any attempt to yoke one's sense of identity and power to one's weaknesses, deficiencies, and perceived victimization. Victimism debilitates its practitioners by trapping them in a world of oppressive demons that they cannot, by definition, control. It is found at the interstices of self-assertion and self-loathing, of moral absolutism and self-doubt.

But victimism's larger sin is its reduction of human experience and the complexity of social relationships to a single monotonic worldview. Blaming one's ills on oppression, on society, on psychological maladjustment, on racism, or on sexism is tempting because those complaints provide clarity and certitude—and perhaps even identity as part of a *faux* community of victims. Such self-diagnoses are perhaps inevitable for a society that has grown unwilling to judge itself in terms of moral order or personal responsibility. But they are also fatally misleading, especially for those members of society who can least afford to indulge in fashionable myths.

Real and Bogus Victims

There are, of course, *real* victims. Neither racism nor sexism are myths; too many men and women continue to experience the injustice of prejudice. The handicapped still face the daunting barriers of everyday life. But here is the rub. The attempt to appropriate the moral qualities of genuine victims for the aggrandizement of less deserving groups and individuals poses no moral or political dilemma for those who refuse to recognize the legitimacy of the real victims. The challenge of the politics of victimization is to those who *do* care about genuine victims and who recognize that victimism reaps its advantage at the direct expense of those most deserving of compassion and support. *If everyone is a victim, then no one is.*

But this purposeful muddling is often a painful thing to acknowledge, especially when the reality of genuine victimization has so powerfully haunted our own times. What child of the 1960s was unaffected by the scenes of beefy white Southern sheriffs beating and bludgeoning peaceful civil rights marchers who had the temerity to ask that they be treated with dignity?

For many of us, it has been easy to judge people simply by whether they have compassion for the underdog. Morality blends imperceptibly into empathy for the downtrodden. So when philosopher John Rawls suggested that no one should ever endorse a social order that he could not accept if he were in the shoes of its most disadvantaged member, he seemed merely to be restating a truism.

If only it were so easy. James Earl Chaney, Andrew Goodman, and Michael Shwerner, the three civil rights workers murdered in Mississippi [in 1964], were obvious martyrs to racism. But what about Washington, D.C., Mayor Marion Barry, who claimed he was a victim of racism after he was caught smoking crack cocaine [in 1990]? . . . It often seems that there is a victimist version of Gresham's Law: Bogus victims drive out genuine victims. [Named (erroneously) after the Elizabethan financier Sir Thomas Gresham, Gresham's Law is that bad money drives out good money.]

Compassion Fatigue

The need to start making careful distinctions between the legitimate objects of compassion and the products of the victimist culture is urgent. Beginning with Rousseau, progressive thinkers have imagined that it is possible to bind a society together not by self-interest but by compassion born out of equality. Victimism, however, has exacted a heavy tax on our compassion and on the sense of guilt that is so integral a part of the politics of victimization.

Americans remain an extraordinarily compassionate people, but it is difficult to escape the sense that we are suffering from compassion fatigue. The excesses of victim politics have generated new skepticism, not only about the more bizarre claims of putative victims but about the very idea that individuals bear moral obligations to the less fortunate. The gridlock of national politics, the refusal of interest groups to surrender their demands to the larger public good, the growing provincialism and parochialism of national politics—all indicate a "What's in it for me?" mentality with troubling consequences for the future.

But if the middle class is truly feeling less guilty, won't victim politics, deprived of that rich source of nutrients, simply wither away in time? No: Victimism's influence is too pervasive. Draining the lake of universal compassion would reveal only the accumulated wreckage of the flight from responsibility and the culture of infinite entitlement. As compassion itself has diminished, society has degenerated into a community of insistent sufferers. What was once conferred compassionately is now demanded by self-proclaimed victims in tones that seem increasingly shrill and meanspirited.

"Instead of dismissing victim stories as individual whining that breeds division and cynicism . . . stories of personal suffering can be used as a means of building public empathy."

Victims' Stories Can Build Compassion in Society

Martha T. McCluskey

Some feminists and other commentators contend that claims of victim status hurt the image of women by portraying them as weak and in need of protection. In the following viewpoint, Martha T. McCluskey maintains that victims' stories can build empathy in American society by giving women and others a voice of authority in public debate. But rather than claiming moral authority based on victimhood, she argues, women should use stories of victimization to provoke debate about the balancing of individual rights and responsibilities. McCluskey is a graduate student and instructor at Columbia University School of Law.

As you read, consider the following questions:

1. According to McCluskey, what determines whether victim stories bolster or harm one's status?
2. According to the author, what is the contrast between speaking about violence against women versus restrictions on fraternities?
3. What does the author say we should do instead of drawing lines between victims and agents?

Martha T. McCluskey, "Transforming Victimization." Reprinted from TIKKUN MAGAZINE, A BIMONTHLY JEWISH CRITIQUE OF POLITICS, CULTURE, AND SOCIETY (March/April 1994). Subscriptions are $31/year from TIKKUN, 251 W. 100th St., 5th Fl., New York, NY 10025. Reproduced by permission of TIKKUN.

Violence against women by middle- or upper-class white men traditionally has been invisible in the public eye. Systematic public denial is the foundation of many of the horrors of modern times. Yet how can we reveal and heal previously hidden injustices, such as domestic violence, acquaintance rape, and sexual harassment, without contributing to the dominant story, which casts women as inevitably damaged and vulnerable to male control? And how can we publicly validate previously silenced personal pain without institutionalizing new forms of unproductive silence?

Instead of dismissing victim stories as individual whining that breeds division and cynicism at worst or paternalistic protection at best, I am interested in how stories of personal suffering can be used as a means of building public empathy.

Victimization and Empowerment

Recently, media attention has focused on the "feminist victimization" problem on college campuses in the context of date-rape education programs and rules governing hate speech and sexual conduct. In this discussion, heterosexual white men at elite colleges are often presented as newly silenced victims of feminist excess and repression. And some people worry that such a focus on women college students as victims of sexual violence will perpetuate antifeminist stereotypes of white, economically privileged women as sexually passive and helpless.

My view is that narratives of women's sexual victimization *can* in some circumstances be used to establish women as empowered and responsible agents. After all, those who identify with privileged male authority have always had it both ways: Our legal system is testament to their success at positioning themselves as both victims and agents. [Supreme Court Justice] Clarence Thomas, for example, achieved his position of supreme public authority [in 1991] through a story of his personal suffering as "high-tech lynching" victim. It is not the subject matter of one's story—victimization—but rather one's position as authoritative subject that determines whether or not narratives of harm bolster or undermine one's power and autonomy. As an example, I'm going to talk about victim stories in one dispute about "political correctness" on college campuses—a lawsuit challenging Colby College's decision to prohibit students from belonging to fraternities.

Colby (a small, selective liberal arts school in Waterville, Maine) banned fraternities and sororities in 1984 as a response to the fraternities' history of sexism, harassment, vandalism, and other problems. In 1990, after six years of continuing problems with fraternities that continued to flourish underground despite the ban, the college punished a group of students for participating in the initiation rituals of a fraternity called Lambda Chi Alpha. The college barred the Lambda Chi seniors from marching in graduation ceremonies and suspended the other members for one semester.

The Maine Civil Liberties Union then initiated a lawsuit on behalf of the punished fraternity members under a new state human rights law. The Civil Liberties Union claimed that the college violated the fraternity members' First Amendment freedom of association rights. In media stories about the lawsuit, the Civil Liberties Union and national fraternity leaders portrayed the fraternity ban as part of a dangerous new wave of intolerance sweeping the country, as colleges force "politically correct" views on students as a result of feminist complaints.

In response, I wrote several essays for local media raising the question of whether some Colby College fraternities might possibly be hate groups in which membership might in some circumstances have the effect of limiting others' equally important freedoms. My essays about the fraternity case were in part a story of my own victimization as a student at Colby. I'm going to repeat a part of my victim story here as an example of the feminist victimization problem. By telling this story, I'm acting out the victim/agency contradiction which I want to transform: I'm positioning myself as silenced victim of misogynist violence and at the same time as speaking author attempting to rewrite the framework within which my victimization is told.

A Story of Victimization

It is 1977 at Colby College. I'm a student living on Third Floor Dana [dormitory]. Most of the guys on our hall are pledging Lambda Chi and KDR, rumored to be the worst fraternities on campus—and the most prestigious.

It's the beginning of a vacation and my dorm is quiet and nearly empty. I am standing in the hallway looking out the window for my ride home. I turn around and my suitcase is gone; Joe and Bill from down the hall are laughing as they carry it away. I follow them. I hear a door lock behind me. They let go of my suitcase and grab me.

I am lying on the bare linoleum floor of Joe's bedroom. In the room are a group of Lambda Chi and KDR pledges who live on my hall; several of them are football players. Some are sitting on the bed, laughing. Two others are pinning my arms and my legs to the floor. Joe is touching me while the others cheer.

I am a friendly fellow-classmate as I reasonably explain that I'm in a rush to catch a ride; that I'm not in the mood to joke around; that I'd really like them to please cut it out. It takes a few long upside-down seconds before things look different. As I start to scream and fight, they let me go.

Later I don't talk about this, not even to myself. I sit near Joe and Bill in sociology and English classes. I don't talk in class.

Victim-vs.-Victim Politics

I used this and other stories of misogynist victimization by Colby fraternity members to try to raise the question of harm to women and other students caused by fraternity membership, a question that had been until then completely left out of the media discussion of the fraternity lawsuit. But the critics of "victim feminism" are right that, interpreted as a confession of my victimization in itself, my story is risky.

The traditional stereotype of certain women as passive sexual victims is inseparable from the traditional stereotype about "other" women as sinister sexual agents. To the extent my victim story is compelling, it reveals my exercise of authority as illegitimately powerful emotional manipulation, while at the same time it shows that I am an emotional, vulnerable female who needs protection from responsible, rigorous debate. Placed within the dominant civil libertarian framework, when I speak about fraternity violence against women, I'm talking about emotional personal experience. In contrast, those who speak about college restrictions on men's right to associate as fraternity brothers are invoking rational universal principles.

The Dual Position of Victims

On the one hand, marginalized groups are now at the discursive center of things—especially in the universities and in the media. Real economic and political power continues to be kept away from traditionally oppressed groups, but in certain circles, cultural clout can come with the status of having been oppressed by "white," "anglo," or "European" dominating forces. On the other hand, to be defined only or essentially as a victim is to be deprived of any agency, and of any history that is not already infected by a dominant group's invasive presence. The position of victim can be powerful when making a claim for justice or redress; the position of victim can be painfully empty when attempting to establish a cultural identity.

Michael S. Roth, *Tikkun*, March/April 1994.

Victim narratives starring privileged heterosexual men are central to establishing the legitimacy of their demands for protection. Reporting on Colby's decision to enforce its ban on fraternities by suspending (not expelling) the members for one semester, a national fraternity leader complained that Colby's president "and his hand-picked thought police regiment have advanced repression to new heights . . . making it a crime punishable by expulsion to be a heterosexual male who chooses to formalize his friendship with other like-minded friends away from campus." Reaching even further, one fraternity member's letter printed in the campus newspaper declared that the college's ban on fraternities was a "form of genocide" comparable to the Holocaust and the Cambodian killing fields.

There's been a flurry of books and media discussions which have widely questioned whether feminists' efforts to stop public denial of sexual violence has led to careless use of the terms "rape" and "sexual harassment." Why isn't there a similarly hot market for books and talk shows urging a heterosexual white male audience to be scrupulously self-critical when they talk about their concerns about feminist tactics?

Indeed, victim narratives by those with social privilege often work to deny responsibility for the social agency that results from that privilege, cleverly making the most privileged people deserving of the greatest legal protection for their suffering. A law journal article cited by fraternity lawyers in the Colby case pointed to evidence of widespread fraternity violence against women as proof that fraternity men suffer from lower self-confidence than college women—suggesting that as a result fraternity men are more disadvantaged and more in need of special legal rights than the women they assault.

The Line Between Victim and Privileged

Critics of "victim feminism" argue that many women shrink from identifying with feminism because of the indignity of the victim role that feminists present. *Newsweek*'s [October 1993] cover story on "Sexual Correctness" on campus acknowledges statistics showing college women are at high risk of sexual assault but then comments: "You want to talk victimization? Talk to the mothers all over America whose children have been slaughtered in urban cross-fire."

Such criticisms tend not to challenge the identification of victims of oppression as pathetic and impotent, but instead aim to simply displace the traditional negative victim image from elite college women onto "others" supposedly distant in terms of race, class, religion, ethnicity, or mental ability. Instead of drawing lines between authentic helpless "victims" and tough empowered "agents," we need to question this dichotomy and recognize that we each share a complicated and contextual mixture of identities of privilege and oppression.

Victim stories alone are not transformative, just as they are not in themselves victimizing. Speaking out about personal pain should be viewed not as an unquestionable revelation of authentic inner experience, but as one honorable way of asserting public power, carrying with it the responsibilities and dangers of such power. By telling my victim story publicly, my goal is not to claim an absolute status as oppressed, nor to inspire apologetic expressions of sympathy or affirmation, but to provoke a rigorous and respectful debate about the line between speech and conduct and to examine the ways perceptions of harm are socially constructed. In order to shape more compassionate and responsible communities with less pain and more pleasure, victim narratives should be a starting point for questioning our assumptions about when we need to accept our fears and our pain as part of giving up privilege and learning to recognize others' sometimes conflicting needs, and when instead we can responsibly demand a community response to our pain as a matter of public principle.

"If we care about attaining a higher level of moral conduct than we now experience, we must be ready to express our moral sense, *raise our moral voice a decibel or two.*"

America's Victim Culture Lacks Moral Values

Amitai Etzioni

Communitarians, who support a liberal political ideology that seeks a balance between civil liberties and civic responsibility, have called for a restoration of moral values in American society to counteract the victimhood trend. In the following viewpoint, Communitarian Network founder Amitai Etzioni argues that a moral reawakening could be accomplished if communities began to lay moral claims on their members. He contends that Americans are too reluctant to voice moral indignation at the offensive behavior of others. Etzioni is the editor of the *Responsive Community*, a quarterly communitarian journal, and author of *The Spirit of Community: Rights, Responsibilities, and the Communitarian Agenda*, from which this viewpoint is excerpted.

As you read, consider the following questions:

1. What is the reason for the moral predicament of American society, in Etzioni's opinion?
2. What examples does the author give of instances where there is no viable community?
3. According to M.P. Baumgartner, cited by the author, what do people often do when they observe offensive conduct?

Excerpted from *The Spirit of Community: Rights, Responsibilities, and the Communitarian Agenda* by Amitai Etzioni (New York: Crown, 1993); ©1993 by Amitai Etzioni. Reprinted by permission of the author.

In the fifties we had a clear set of values that spoke to most Americans, most of the time, with a firm voice. These values were often discriminatory against women (who were not allowed into many clubs, to have credit in their own name, or to advance far in their jobs) and against minorities, from blacks to Jews. They were also at least a bit authoritarian. When your doctor told you that you needed surgery, you did not even think of asking for a second opinion. When your boss ordered you around at work, you did not mention that the Japanese invite their workers to participate in decision making. When your priest, labor leader, or father spoke, he spoke with authority. Indeed, often such figures of authority expected unquestioning obedience. . . .

The State of the Union's Morality

In the sixties all these voices and the values they spoke for were deeply challenged—as they ought to have been. That challenge, though, is *not* the reason for the moral predicament we find ourselves in these days in both private and public realms. The problem is that the waning of traditional values was not followed by a solid affirmation of new values; often nothing filled the empty spaces that were left when we razed existing institutions. The result is rampant moral confusion and social anarchy. We often cannot tell right from wrong—or cannot back up what we do believe in. Thus, while traditional authority figures were challenged, the new form of "participatory democracy" that was supposed to replace them remained largely a vague slogan. Above all, the young these days are bombarded with incessant violent, sexual, and commercial messages, but they hear relatively few credible, morally reaffirming voices.

The eighties tried to turn vice into virtue by elevating the unbridled pursuit of self-interest and greed to the level of social virtue. It turned out that an *economy* could thrive (at least for a while) if people watched out only for themselves (although this is by no means as well documented as many economists suggest, and it is certainly not what the classic economist Adam Smith favored). But it has become evident that a *society* cannot function well given such self-centered, me-istic orientations. It requires a set of dos and don'ts, a set of moral values, that guides people toward what is decent and encourages them to avoid that which is not.

I often ask my students whether if they had a severe cash shortfall—in plain English, if they needed money badly—they would consider selling a kidney (the going price is about $10,000 in Europe). They look at me as if the old man has finally lost his senses, and I am proud of them. Their reaction is what we require in more areas. *We need to return to a society in which certain*

30

actions are viewed as beyond the pale, things that upright people would not do or even consider: to walk out on their children, file false insurance claims, cheat on tests, empty the savings accounts of others, or force sexual advances on unwilling employees. We also need to return to a state in which there are a fair number of positive compelling commitments—the dos rather than the don'ts—that are beyond debate and dispute. When a sick child cries at night, a parent rushes to help. There is no need to consult clergy or a book by Immanuel Kant to determine what one's duty is under such clear, elementary conditions. This is what Alexis de Tocqueville and Communitarian sociologist Robert Bellah mean by "habits of the heart": values that command our support because they are morally compelling.

Individual and Group Morality

At least in the Western tradition, morality has always depended upon a notion of individual responsibility or accountability, but it has always been established collectively by the group. In the strict sense, individual morality in isolation is meaningless. An individual is moral only in the measure that he or she conforms to the prevailing standards of a community, which means in the measure that he or she observes some fundamental rules, which means in the measure that he or she accepts some authority beyond the individual. "I want," or even "I believe," much less, "I feel," does not morality make. Yes, the Western (Judeo-Christian) tradition has always included space for the individual who refuses to conform to the standards of the group in the name of a higher morality, but such righteous rebellions have been launched in the name of a higher authority, not personal convenience.

Elizabeth Fox-Genovese, *Tikkun*, March/April 1994.

Communitarians do not suggest that we return to the traditional values of the fifties. We do not favor, say, a return to the "Leave It to Beaver" family (the father at work, the mother shut in the kitchen), but to a communitarian family—one in which both parents are actively and deeply involved in their children's upbringing. Similarly, Communitarians favor not a return to authoritarian leadership, but a climate that fosters finding agreed-upon positions that we can favor authoritatively.

We do require a set of social virtues, some basic settled values, that we as a community endorse and actively affirm. Thus, if we are to maintain our edge in an increasingly competitive world, workers will have to come to their jobs drug free and sober, stay sober all the time they are on the job, and give a day's work for a decent day's pay. We must reaffirm that expressions of hate toward members of other ethnic or racial groups, not to mention violent behavior, are intolerable. And although we may disagree on exactly how far we should go in protecting our shared environment (for example, what rights do spotted owls have?), we will most certainly express our disapproval of those who flush their engine oil down the drain, refuse to sort their garbage, or wash their cars and water their lawns when the town's water reservoir is low and falling. At the same time, we will continue to debate other values that are contested, seek changes in the prevailing consensus, and even rebel if we feel we are pushed too far, by moral claims or a choir of our peers. . . .

The Community as a Moral Voice

How can the moral voice of the community function when it is well articulated and clearly raised?

I lived for a year on the Stanford University campus. Not far from the house I rented was a four-way stop sign. Each morning I observed a fairly heavy flow of traffic at the intersection. Still, the cars carefully waited their turns to move ahead, as they were expected to. The drivers rarely moved out of turn, and in those cases when they did, the offenders often had out-of-state license plates. The main reason for the good conduct: practically everyone in the community knew who was behind the wheel. If someone rushed through, he or she could expect to be the subject of some mild ribbing at the faculty club, supermarket, or local movie theater (such as "You must have been in an awful rush this morning"). This kind of community prodding usually suffices to reinforce the proper behavior that members of the community acquire early—in this case, observing safe traffic patterns.

When I first moved to a suburb of Washington, D.C., I neglected to mow my lawn. One neighbor asked politely if I needed "a reference to a good gardener." Another pointed out that unless we all kept up the standards of the neighborhood, we would end up with an unsightly place and declining property values. Soon after I moved into a downtown cooperative building, the tenants were sent memos that reminded us to sort our garbage. Various exhortations were used ("It is good for the environment"), and a floor representative was appointed to "oversee" compliance. I never found out what the representative actually did; the very appointment and reminders seemed sufficient for most residents to attend to their trash properly.

It might be said that I have lived in middle-class parts. It is well established, however, that many working-class and immigrant communities—to the extent that they are intact—uphold their values. These are often further modulated and backed up by the ethnic groups. Thus the specific values may differ from a Cuban to an Irish neighborhood, or from an Asian to a black one, but all communities sustain values. Their concerns may vary from what is the proper way to conduct a wake or a confirmation to how much help a new immigrant can expect or whether a local shopkeeper will hire illegal aliens. But it is mainly in instances in which there is no viable community, in which people live in high-rise buildings and do not know one another, in some city parts in which the social fabric is frayed, and in situations in which people move around a lot and lose most social moorings, that the social underpinnings of morality are lost.

How to Win Friends?

The examples of moral voices that carry that I have cited so far are about matters of limited importance, such as lawns and garbage. Hence, community responses to those who disregard the shared values have been appropriately mild. When people misbehave in more serious ways, the community's response tends to be stronger, especially when the community is clear about what is right and wrong. If someone's child speeds down the street as though there were no tomorrow or throws beer bottles at passersby, the rebuke is appropriately sharper. People may say to parents, "We are all deeply troubled about what happened the other day when you were not home" or "For the sake of the safety of all of us, we [meaning you] must find a way to ensure that this will not happen again." Basketball star David Robinson once explained to a TV interviewer that instead of telling everybody that "you are great," he "gets into the face" of those who need to be told right from wrong. Americans brought up on Dale Carnegie [author of *How to Win Friends and Influence People*], anxious never to give offense, may find such an approach a bit moralistic. Well, as I see it, *what we need now is less "how to win friends and influence people" and more how to restore the sway of moral voices.*

Most important, the moral voice does not merely censure; it also blesses. We appreciate, praise, recognize, celebrate, and toast those who serve their communities, from volunteer fire fighters to organizers of neighborhood crime watches. Members of a neighborhood constantly share tales of how wonderful it was that this or that individual organized a group to take care of the trees on the side of the road, rushed to welcome the new families that escaped from Iran, or whatever. It is these positive, fostering, encouraging, yet effective moral voices that we no longer hear with sufficient clarity and conviction in many areas of our lives.

Often when I speak about the need to shore up the moral

voice of our communities, I observe a sense of unease. Americans do not like to tell other people how to behave. I first ran into the fear many liberal people have of formulating and expressing moral claims, of articulating the moral voice of the community, when I taught at Harvard. A faculty seminar was conducted on the ethical condition of America. The first session was dedicated to a discussion of what our agenda should be. I suggested a discussion of the moral implications of the decline of the American family. Nobody objected, but nobody picked up on the idea, either; it was politely but roundly ignored. When I later asked two members of the seminar why my suggestion had been accorded such a quiet burial, they explained that they (and presumably other members of the seminar) were uncomfortable discussing the subject. "If a high-profile group of ethicists at Harvard would form a consensus on the matter, it might put a lot of pressure on people, and it might even be used to change the laws [on divorce]."

The Fear of Moral Claims

Sociologist M.P. Baumgartner found that in an American suburb he studied in the 1980s, people who observed minor violations of conduct often simply ignored them rather than express their displeasure. If the violations were somewhat serious, people tended to ostracize the offenders without explanation. If they did confront a miscreant—say, a person who burned chicken feathers in his backyard and stank up the neighborhood, mowed the lawn early in the morning, or left a barking dog out at night—they were likely to ask him to cease the behavior as a *favor* to them, rather than labeling it as something a decent person would not do.

This disinclination to lay moral claims undermines the daily, routine social underwriting of morality. It also hinders moral conduct in rather crucial situations.

During a conference on bone-marrow transplants, a psychiatrist argued that it was not proper to ask one sibling for a bone-marrow donation for another sibling, despite the fact that making such a donation does not entail any particular risk. His reason was that the sibling who refused might feel guilty, especially if as a result the brother or sister died. On the contrary, a Communitarian would argue that siblings should be asked in no uncertain terms to come to the rescue. If they refuse, they *should* feel guilty.

When I discuss the value of moral voices, people tell me they are very concerned that if they lay moral claims, they will be perceived as self-righteous. If they mean by "self-righteous" a person who comes across as without flaw, who sees himself as entitled to dictate what is right (and wrong), who lays moral

34

claims in a sanctimonious or pompous way—there is good reason to refrain from such ways of expressing moral voices. But these are secondary issues that involve questions of proper expressions and manner of speech.

At the same time we should note that given our circumstances, our society would be much better off if some of its members sometimes erred on the side of self-righteousness (on which they are sure to be called) than be full of people who are morally immobilized by a fear of being considered prudish or members of a "thought police." . . . I realize that when I speak of the value of the two-parent family, many of my single-parent friends frown. I do not mean to put them down, but their displeasure should not stop me or anybody else from reporting what we see as truthful observations and from drawing morally appropriate conclusions. It is my contention that *if we care about attaining a higher level of moral conduct than we now experience, we must be ready to express our moral sense,* raise our moral voice a decibel or two. In the silence that prevails, it may seem as if we are shouting; actually we are merely speaking up.

Toward a Moral Community

As more and more of us respond to the claims that we ought to assume more responsibilities for our children, elderly, neighbors, environment, and communities, moral values will find more support. Although it may be true that markets work best if everybody goes out and tries to maximize his or her own self-interest (although that is by no means a well-proven proposition), moral behavior and communities most assuredly do not. They require people who care for one another and for shared spaces, causes, and future. Here, clearly, it is better to give than to take, and the best way to help sustain a world in which people care for one another—is to care for some. The best way to ensure that common needs are attended to is to take some responsibility for attending to some of them.

To object to the moral voice of the community, and to the moral encouragement it provides, is to oppose the social glue that helps hold the moral order together. It is unrealistic to rely on individuals' inner voices and to expect that people will invariably do what is right completely on their own. Such a radical individualistic view disregards our social moorings and the important role that communities play in sustaining moral commitments. Those who oppose statism must recognize that communities require some ways of making their needs felt. They should welcome the gentle, informal, and—in contemporary America—generally tolerant voices of the community, especially given that the alternative is typically state coercion or social and moral anarchy.

"We have become a nation of meddlers."

America's Victim Culture Is Overly Moralistic

Charles Edgley and Dennis Brissett

Some social critics have noted, along with the rise of victimhood in American society, the rise of groups of concerned citizens who express an increasingly vocal intolerance of "offensive" behaviors. In the following viewpoint, Charles Edgley and Dennis Brissett argue that attempts by some to control the behavior of others are unwelcome and impertinent intrusions and are not an effective way to restore community morality to American society. The authors advocate a return to the social virtues of tolerance of others and minding one's own business. Edgley is a professor of sociology at Oklahoma State University in Stillwater. Brissett is a professor of behavioral science at the University of Minnesota Medical School in Duluth.

As you read, consider the following questions:

1. What is the definition of meddling offered by Edgley and Brissett?
2. How does H.G. Wells, cited by the authors, define moral indignation?
3. What are the two hallmarks of minding one's own business, according to the authors?

There was a time long ago when the phrase "it's none of your business" meant something. Not any more. A boorish and persistent army of meddlers, equipped with righteous indignation and a formidable array of theories and technologies, has made almost everyone's business its own. Meddling in the lives of others is now the republic's most visible obsession. Examples are everywhere—from national crusades against bad habits such as drinking, smoking, and gambling to the efforts of a group in Woodbury, Minnesota, to create a "fragrance-free" work environment where workers are insulated not only from the disgusting stench of tobacco smoke but also from the aroma of perfumes, shampoos, and aftershave lotion as well. In Phoenix, Arizona, the city council passed a law requiring installation of a swimming pool to be accompanied by child-proofing any access from the house to the pool, even if no children reside in the house. In Flossmoor, Illinois, the town council invoked an ancient ordinance outlawing pickup trucks because their image is "inconsistent with residential living." In Tacoma Park, Maryland, a group of "concerned citizens" tried to ban outdoor grills and lawn mowers, spawning a countermovement that calls itself "pro-choice" on the question of charcoal and Toros. Surveillance efforts by employers, such as electronically monitoring a computer operator's keystrokes per minute, videotaping production lines, and timing employee visits to the bathroom, seem all too commonplace.

A Nation of Meddlers

While a certain amount of meddling seems endemic to human association, the historical record indicates that in former times meddling was perpetrated almost exclusively in terms of widely agreed upon precepts of public morality and civic duty. Such moral and civic meddling, while often resented, was at least expected and was confined primarily to legitimate authorities and institutions. Other persons who meddled, such as gossips, snoops, and assorted amateur practitioners of the meddling trade, have always been high on the list of public nuisances. But the quantum leap in meddling came in the last half century, when there was added to this roster full-time practitioners who actually made a living meddling into other people's lives. As Philip Rieff has described it, this "triumph of the therapeutic" resulted in a proliferation of professional meddlers. Even H.L. Mencken, that dogged critic of the meddlesome impulse (who complained that "every third American devotes himself to improving and uplifting his fellow-citizen, usually by force"), might be surprised if he were around to see how much more that impulse rules the country now than it did at the turn of the century. We meddle in the name of almost everything: health, safety, efficiency, the bottom line, God, "the children"—you name it, we meddle on its behalf. We are at the ready to meddle with most anyone who crosses either our path or our vested interests. We now meddle with just about anything people do as long as it happens to be something we ourselves do not do. We have become a nation of meddlers. . . .

Defining Meddling

A century ago it would have been unnecessary to define meddling—everyone knew what it was and denounced it roundly. Since the term has fallen into disuse, a fresh definition is in order—to wit: Meddling involves a thrusting of oneself, often boldly, into the affairs of others. Meddlesome acts are those that impertinently and promiscuously tamper with that which, under usual and ordinary circumstances, would not be considered within the domain of the meddler. Meddling, then, can range from simple nosiness or eavesdropping to the offering of services or attention to outright interference in other people's lives. Meddlesome acts are intrusions or obtrusions that invade what is ordinarily considered to be another's private world. It is the very power of the meddler to convert the usual into the unusual and the ordinary into the extraordinary that allows the private realm of the meddlee to be viewed as a public arena susceptible to, indeed requiring, meddlesome intervention. So in a fundamental sense, meddling involves an appropriation of and a proprietorship over the heretofore private matters of another, whether these be matters of word, deed, or thought. No matter the subject of the meddling, or the manner in which it is done, meddling implies that the meddlee is not comporting him- or herself as he or she might. Nevertheless, from the point of view of the meddlee, most meddling is seen, at least initially, as unwelcome, if not downright improper, and certainly unnecessary, annoying, or offensive. . . .

Meddling and Community Spirit

Obviously, not all this meddling is bad. In fact, the consequences of meddling, at least in terms of what the meddler wishes to accomplish may be quite positive. But whether meddlesome interventions succeed or not (and there always seems a way to make them seem successful), a deeper concern is the attitude of meddling that has become so prevalent in our society. Increasingly, it seems, people are stampeded into believing, with very little reflection and much cocksure arrogance about the matter, that meddling and being meddled with are cultural virtues; indeed, that they are the hallmark of what good people do for each other. The alternative to meddling is now more often seen as an apathetic, uncaring, isolated disregard for others symbolized by those tragic instances in which cries for help go unheard or unanswered. Meddling presumably alters this apathetic scenario by demonstrating one's "concern." Still, while apathy and isolation certainly may be problems, it seems to us that the solution to them does not reside in the meddlesome acts that now pass for community spirit and social involvement.

An even more pernicious dimension is, however, at the nub of meddling. It is that meddling is done so impertinently. It is the meddler's impudent arrogance, effrontery, and audacious presumptive understanding of the meddlee that makes meddling so different from most other forms of human association. Meddlers neither approve nor indulge the meddlee's behavior. At the same time, they presume to understand—or at least claim to be in possession of an understanding of how to understand—not just the behavior but the self, relationships, and entire life of the meddlee. In short, it is the meddlers wholesale, know-it-all arrogation of the meddlee that makes meddling the bane of modern civilization. In the process, differences between the meddler and meddlee become inequalities, establishing the moral, intellectual, and psychological superiority of the meddler. As Alida Brill, author of *Nobody's Business: Paradoxes of Privacy*, has observed, "privacy invasions are virtually always justified for a higher moral purpose or public good or for a nobler motivation than privacy protection." So it is little wonder that people take such pride in being meddlers. It just may be the last bastion of socially sanctioned snobbery in an egalitarian society. . . .

The Other Side of Community

Intrusions into people's lives in the name of God and those on behalf of the magic words "health" and "safety" give us some insight into why people meddle, but the kind of meddling that emerges from the currently fashionable solution to the age-old antagonism between individualism and community tells us even more. This resolution to what Brill has called "this eternal conflict between the belief in the inherent worth and good of personal and individual freedom versus the belief in regulation and control of others' lives for the presumed public good" has occasioned a rather peculiar vision of what constitutes a "proper" public order. Owing perhaps to the seriously diminished opportunities for either formal political participation or a thriving informal public sociability, people have turned to controlling others as an acceptable and even laudable form of public participation. The lonely void of a self-possessed individualism poignantly noted by so many of Robert Bellah's respondents in *Habits of the Heart* seems to have been resolved for many people in a most unusual way. Meddling has become their attempt at connection with others. But in the process of reaching out to others they neglect the other side of community, which involves and even requires a certain civil tolerance, if not an active appreciation of diverse others—a sentiment that depends so much on what Tennessee Williams calls the "kindness of strangers."

Reprinted by permission of Chuck Asay and Creators Syndicate.

Moreover, as we seek community through meddling with others, a proper distinction between privacy and secrecy becomes hopelessly confused or even obliterated. For as Sissela Bok has commented, privacy, or "the condition of being protected from unwanted access by others—either physical access or personal information or attention," is far different from secrecy or "intentional concealment." But in the consciousness of a nation of meddlers, appeals to privacy are construed as pernicious efforts to conceal matters that undermine the public good. They are seen as symptomatic expressions of the new-found sin of keeping one's own counsel. The commonweal, it is said, depends on everything being out in the open, and if people have something they wish to keep private, they must be up to no good. So in the name of a misguided sense of community, the whole of life, particularly those aspects that others wish to keep private, becomes open to the meddler's gaze. The irony, of course, is that those persons who seek community through meddling are themselves engaging in a kind of politics of exclusion. For it is not interaction or mutuality or even "knowledge of" others that they seek,

40

but rather a self-aggrandizing control or influence over others based on "knowledge about" them; hardly the stuff or fabric of community, but rather more akin to the social world of gossips, snoops, and busybodies. So in one very important sense, meddling is individualism masquerading as community. It is difficult to tell whether altruism, caring, and honest concern are as much the *goals* of meddling as they are simply the high-minded *justifications* that serve to disguise the meddler's self-interest as philanthropic, public spirited, and humanitarian. What seems sacred in meddling is not the doing of good works, but rather the sense of personal accomplishment derived from the meddling act itself. But because we take meddling into each other's affairs as a sure sign of community-mindedness, we may well have reached a point where, as Wendy Kaminer has observed, "never have so many known so much about people for whom they care so little."

Meddling and Moral Indignation

A proper account of the meddling impulse must also recognize that meddling is often accompanied by a certain moral indignation, and while there may be much to be legitimately indignant about, it must also be remembered that moral indignation has much within it that is reminiscent of H.G. Wells's definition: "jealousy with a halo." Svend Ranulf, author of *Moral Indignation and Middle Class Psychology*, among others less careful and profound, has pointed out that, like other middle-class social movements, much moral indignation betrays a certain disguised envy. This murderous sentiment (one of the seven deadly sins explicated so nicely by Stanford Lyman, author of *The Seven Deadly Sins*) attempts to punish, rather than merely comment upon, those departures from the virtue so staunchly supported by the meddler. Reforming the morals of others is clearly one way in which groups act to preserve the dominance and prestige of their own lifestyles. Even the slightest pique of resentment about others doing what meddlers feel they themselves should not, or cannot, do often seems like a quick and compelling reason to meddle into these other people's lives. Moreover, for the increasing number of Americans who are dissatisfied or bored with their all-too-proper lives, meddling offers the promise of reaffirming a sense of efficacy and credibility in a world that seems so often to be totally out of control. Moral indignation is a powerful intoxicant—to say nothing of a vicarious stimulant— for the weary and jaded who object to the raft of unsuitable enjoyments and pleasures of their fellow citizens. And while Lionel Tiger's observation (in *The Pursuit of Pleasure*) that "powerful people enjoy it when they are able to define and restrict the pleasures of others" is undoubtedly true, it is also true that certain people enjoy power by virtue of their being able to define and restrict others' pleasure. . . .

Toward a Less Meddlesome Society

We might . . . try to practice a good deal more forbearance in our dealings with one another. Americans have always been wary of strangers, but we seem to be increasingly suspicious of our friends, neighbors, and acquaintances as well. The postmodern indiscriminate sensitivity to the foibles, mistakes, and offenses of others has occasioned a pandemic of fault finding. When things go wrong, as they so often do, our overriding concern has become one of finding what, or more often who, is at fault. While this mechanistic logic may be suitable to the high-tech investigation of plane crashes, it seems pathetically misguided when applied to the age-old conundrums of life. But goaded as we are by the scientific persuasion that whatever bad things happen are a consequence of the preventable conditions that preceded them, Americans have become a mercilessly accusatory lot. Our belief in the promise of a trouble-free life seems preserved and rationalized by the persistent identification of those persons who would make trouble for the rest of us. Nirvana is within our grasp, we seem to be saying, if only we could educate, rehabilitate, or treat these troublemakers. So we meddle, seemingly oblivious to the possibility that life may just be that proverbial "vale of tears," or at the very least an imperfect juxtaposition of human frailty and power. If we must meddle, we might consider appreciating and acting upon such old-fashioned sentiments as "putting up with" and "learning to live with"—hallmarks of minding one's own business. We might even become reacquainted with that central communal gift of sometimes ignoring those things with which we disagree or find offensive. For it seems to us that in the long run, reasonable tolerance, not reasoned intolerance, is the far more essential component in sustaining both human relationships and communities. . . .

The righteous attitude that so often attends an absolutist stance toward other people's lives seems to occasion not only an insensitivity but also a rudeness in human affairs. As columnist and author Judith Martin observes, "the moral virtue of devotion to the well-being of others supposedly obliterates the rule of etiquette against minding other people's business." In a society where moral rectitude is valued over common courtesy, she says, nosiness is justified as curiosity:

> In those rare instances nowadays, when someone who asks personal questions is taxed with invasion of privacy, the offender points out he was simply wondering or "interested in" what another paid for his house, why he uses a wheelchair, or whether he is planning to get a divorce.

42

When meddlers armed with righteousness become not only curious but also proactive, any sense of mannerly interaction is subordinated to the meddler's cause, whether he or she is a proponent of clean air, clean talk, clean sex, or clean breath. We agree with Judith Martin that it is time to reexamine the social cost exacted by a society of moral and legal absolutists who have forgotten, if they ever knew, that the oldest virtues of communal harmony, cultural coherence, and dignity of the person derive far more from our practiced civility with one another than they do from our attempts to frighten, harass, and coerce each other into not doing whatever it is we don't like.

*"Political correctness may be paved with good
intentions, but so is the road to Hades."*

Political Correctness
Denigrates American
Culture

Gerald F. Kreyche

Political correctness, a movement to eliminate speech and actions that are considered demeaning to women and minorities,
has been criticized by its opponents for inhibiting free speech
and communication. In the following viewpoint, Gerald F. Kreyche contends that the movement has had a detrimental effect in
many areas of life, including newspapers, the law, museums,
and education. He argues that political correctness, by focusing
on America's faults instead of its achievements, distorts the
truth. Kreyche is an editor of *USA Today* magazine.

As you read, consider the following questions:

1. According to Kreyche, why is political correctness about
   actions more than words?
2. What was John Leo's criticism of the Smithsonian museum
   display, according to the author?

Gerald F. Kreyche, "Political Correctness: Speech Control or Thought Control?" *USA Today*
magazine, March 1995; © by the Society for the Advancement of Education. Reprinted with
permission.

The *Random House Dictionary* defines political correctness as "marked by or adhering to a typically progressive orthodoxy on issues involving especially race, gender, sexual affinity or ecology." This definition certainly covers a multitude of sins committed by nonadherents of PC. Let's look at these sins of omission and commission.

When political correctness started out, many thought it was an academic joke, referring to taxation as "revenue enhancement" or the handicapped as "physically challenged." Many even thought articles concerning PC were about personal computers and skipped reading them. Some, such as syndicated columnist Ed Quillen, did a bit of nose-thumbing by illustrating the absurdity if carried to its full implications. He suggested the banning of real estate advertising using terms such as "master bedroom," a "walk-in closet" (as offensive to wheelchair-bound buyers), and "spectacular views" (to placate the blind).

Political Correctness in the Media

However, when the Scrabble dictionary eliminated nearly one hundred time-honored words deemed to be nonpolitically correct, people knew that PC was picking up a head of steam. The *Los Angeles Times* issued guidelines for its writers that prohibited ("discouraged," to be PC) the use of a number of words. Among them were "man-made," no doubt a fop to feminists, "Dutch treat," "ghetto," "inner city," "Hispanic," and "Indian." One suspects that the *Times* was influenced heavily by the French Parliament's banning of 3,500 words, mostly Americanisms such as "cheeseburger," "chewing gum," and "bulldozer." The English, tongue in cheek, then threatened to ban French words such as "laissez-faire."

Even sign language has felt the revisionism of the correctness movement. Black now is signed not by putting two fingers on one's nose, but by the letter "A" circling the face (for Afro-American). The former sign for Indian as showing two fingers (representing feathers) behind one's head also is changed. A gay person no longer is signed by a flip of the wrist, but by the letter "G."

Political correctness is not so much about words, as it is about action and conduct, for words lead from ideas into real life. In North Carolina, for instance, a judge remarked of a female attorney defending someone accused of robbery that he didn't like to argue with a "pretty girl." The result was a Supreme Court decision requiring a new trial for her client. In Dallas, Texas, after a trial involving a man convicted of raping a lesbian, the bailiff said in an aside that, instead of the long sentence handed out, if he were judge, he only would give thirty days. That cost the bailiff a ten-day suspension and a loss of $842 in pay.

Near St. George, Utah, two tortoises on the endangered species list accidentally were killed during construction of an arts complex. The Department of Justice fined the sponsor, the Heritage Arts Foundation, $20,000. Two workers, finding a dead tortoise, planted one at the construction site and promptly were fired for their insensitive prank. Humorist Garrison Keillor is right—nobody can take a joke today.

Politically Correct History

The venerable Smithsonian Institution was caught up in the throes of the political correctness controversy. John Leo, an editorial writer for *U.S. News and World Report*, hammered away mercilessly at them about the institution's original plans for an *Enola Gay* display of the [August 1945] atomic bombing of Japan that accused Americans of being racists and imperialists. In addition, he charged that it deprecated American heroes as historical elitists, while praising Japanese kamikaze pilots. The Smithsonian ultimately pared the exhibition to duck the controversy.

Political Correctness Is Not the Answer

Just as language grotesquely inflates in attack, so it timidly shrinks in approbation, seeking words that cannot possibly give any offense, however notional. We do not fail, we underachieve. We are not junkies, but substance abusers; not handicapped, but differently abled. And we are mealy-mouthed unto death: a corpse, the *New England Journal of Medicine* urged in 1988, should be referred to as a "nonliving person." By extension, a fat corpse is a differently sized nonliving person.

If these affected contortions actually made people treat one another with more civility and understanding, there might be an argument for them. But they do no such thing.

Robert Hughes, *Culture of Complaint*, 1993.

One thing leads to another in the PC movement. The nation now is being sold guidelines to what might be called "affirmative action teaching" in the new 279-page book, *United States History: Exploring the American Experience*. This is supposed to revolutionize the teaching of history, and indeed it will, for it is viewed as essentially negative toward American heroes; concentrates on the country's warts, rather than its achievements; and sings the praises of women and minorities, who seem to be without relative fault. No mention is made of Paul Revere, the Wright brothers, or Thomas Edison. Ulysses S. Grant is given one citation only, but Joseph McCarthy and McCarthyism are cited nineteen times, and the Ku Klux Klan seventeen. Native Americans become *noble* again, ignoring many tribes who took slaves, committed hideous tortures, and treated their wives as chattel, beat them, cut off their noses for adultery, and gambled them away.

Political correctness may be paved with good intentions, but so is the road to Hades. It not only hides truth, but denies it. PC insinuates untruth and sacrifices truth for compromise. It has spawned Afrocentric education, which has taken root in places as disparate as Portland, Oregon, and New York City. It charges that Greek philosophy (the basis of Western thinking) was stolen from Africa. Many black teachers make claims that melanin (which makes the skin darker) confers superior intelligence. Charles Murray and Richard Herrnstein's controversial book, *The Bell Curve*, currently is taking that notion to task.

One suspects that backers of political correctness, also known as the "word police," would like to graduate to "thought police." Those who didn't conform would undergo re-education, as do many faculty members accused of insensitivity in the classroom.

In the end, political correctness is only self-serving as it celebrates the coming of the multicultural revolution. The national motto will be changed from *E pluribus unum* to *In diversis fiat unitas* (unity is made from diversity). All values, such as lifestyles, will be equally valuable. Unfortunately for the PC people, though, their program is flawed and, ultimately, reality will have its way.

"What other way is there to make change other than to raise a stink when you see something that makes you angry?"

Political Correctness Challenges America's Oppressive Culture

Andrea Lewis

The political correctness movement seeks to curb the use of certain words and stereotypes that are considered offensive by women and minorities. In the following viewpoint, Andrea Lewis argues that even though political correctness provides no immediate benefit to women and minorities, the movement has raised awareness of how offensive speech and stereotypes can adversely affect them. Lewis is a contributing editor of *Third Force*, a bimonthly magazine on issues in communities of color.

As you read, consider the following questions:

1. What is the criticism of political correctness made by "those on the left," according to Lewis?
2. What is the effect of political correctness on mainstream culture and television, according to *Time* magazine, as quoted by the author?
3. What does the author say *Time* is really doing when it uses the label "politically correct"?

Andrea Lewis, "P.C. or Not to Be," *Third Force*, vol. 1, no. 6, January/February 1994. Reprinted by permission of *Third Force*.

If there's one thing that the left, the middle and the right seem to agree on, it's hating political correctness. The middle and the right wings view p.c. as neo-fascist mind control. Those on the left view being politically correct as a lazy and reactionary approach to political action, and use it to refer to people who talk a good progressive political line but are too afraid to get their hands dirty with the real political work.

Nobody will cop to the label. So who is pushing this politically correct agenda that we keep hearing about? The term is so prevalent that you'd think there was a thundering horde of armchair activists out there, demanding p.c. behavior without respect for the First Amendment and basically being a pain in the ass to "real Americans."

Media Bashing of Political Correctness

Time magazine feels that they've nailed down the culprits. They tried to get a handle on the p.c. horde in their October 25, 1993, article on the backlash against p.c. The article, in *Time's* typically sweeping style of cultural analysis, went so far as to indict proponents of political correctness for giving the world Rush Limbaugh, Howard Stern, and Beavis & Butthead. . . . "The guardians of political correctness—the careful laundering of speech, actions and school textbooks to avoid offending women, ethnic groups and other minorities—have been riding high in recent years," *Time* explains. A few lines later, they report that these "guardians" or "p.c. police" have caused mainstream culture to "become cautious, sanitized, scared of its own shadow. Network TV, targeted by antiviolence crusaders and nervous about offending advertisers, has purged itself of what little edge and controversy it once had."

With one deft keystroke, *Time* has managed to cut and paste together progressive watchdog groups like the Arab-American Anti-Discrimination Committee with Christian fundamentalist groups like Donald Wildmon's American Family Association, who pressure the media to broadcast and support only traditional American family values.

It's ironic that *Time* accuses "women, ethnic groups, and other minorities" of sanitizing mainstream culture, when members of those very groups say that it is they who have been "whitewashed" out of our cultural history. It's equally ironic to look into the most reactionary, anti-p.c. mouths that roar. Yes it's true. Rush Limbaugh and Howard Stern are two white guys. Hummmm.

In the unending media flogging of poor little p.c., no one, including *Time* magazine, takes the time to make any connections between our culture's oppressive and exclusionary history and today's movements aimed at raising consciousness about media

49

language and images.

After decades of enduring widely-circulated jokes, stereotyped television and film characters, caricatures, and basically being the ever-present butt of humor in the mainstream culture of our society, it's difficult for members of disenfranchised communities (people of color, women, lesbians and gay men, the differently abled, people of lower income, etc.) to be anything less than thin-skinned. What other way is there to make change other than to raise a stink when you see something that makes you angry?

"P.C." Debate Prevents Real Debate

P.C. is a menace, but perhaps for different reasons than the other side would say. It's a menace because it obscures the real problems and issues that we face as a society. It's a clever rhetorical phrase which turns a debate about racism and sexism into a debate about censorship.

If you can force us to discuss censorship instead of discussing racial epithets, censorship instead of discussing sexual harassment, censorship instead of discussing the question how we are going to transform our institutions into more diverse places, then you have set the terms of the debate and prevented a discussion of the real issues.

Linda S. Greene, *New York Times*, December 11, 1993.

Unfortunately, we don't have a Department of Speech and Ethics to determine once and for all whether or not the official term should be "disabled" or "differently abled" or "physically challenged." Should it be gay/lesbian/bisexual or queer? Should Black become African American? How exactly do we define sexual harassment? How do we discourage racial epithets and hate speech without violating the spirit of the First Amendment? The only way to debate these issues is to hash them out in public. When *Time* labels anyone who raises these topics "politically correct," what the editors are really doing is shifting the debate from the question at hand to questioning the motives of the person or group who raised the issue in the first place. . . .

Protesting unbalanced images of criminals of color, Muslim terrorists, lesbian psycho-killers and other stupid stereotypes may not make any immediate change in anyone's standard of living. But discussing these subjects does get people to think and talk about the power of cultural images, and the profound ways that they affect our identities, perceptions and actions.

Periodical Bibliography

The following articles have been selected to supplement the diverse views presented in this chapter. Addresses are provided for periodicals not indexed in the *Readers' Guide to Periodical Literature*, the *Alternative Press Index*, or the *Social Sciences Index*.

Jesse Birnbaum	"Crybabies: Eternal Victims," *Time*, August 12, 1991.
Sarah Crichton	"Sexual Correctness: Has It Gone Too Far?" *Newsweek*, October 25, 1993.
John Elson	"Busybodies: New Puritans," *Time*, August 12, 1991.
Elizabeth Fox-Genovese	"The State of Contemporary Politics and Culture," *Tikkun*, March/April 1994.
Pete Hamill	"End Game," *Esquire*, December 1994.
Robert Hughes	"The Fraying of America," *Time*, February 3, 1992.
Jonathan B. Imber	"American Therapies and Pieties," *American Enterprise*, May/June 1993. Available from 1150 17th St. NW, Washington, DC 20036.
John Lewis, Andrea Dworkin, and Merle Hoffman	"Towards a Revolution in Values," *On the Issues*, Fall 1994.
Walter A. McDougall	"Whose History? Whose Standards?" *Commentary*, May 1995.
Louis Menand	"The War of All Against All," *New Yorker*, March 14, 1994.
Lance Morrow	"A Nation of Finger Pointers," *Time*, August 12, 1991.
Roger Rosenblatt	"Who Killed Privacy? The Right to Know Everything About Everybody," *New York Times Magazine*, January 31, 1993.
Manfred Stanley	"Political Correctness: On How to Begin the Debate," *Higher Education Exchange*, 1994. Available from 200 Commons Rd., Dayton, OH 45459.
Jon Wiener	"History Lesson," *New Republic*, January 2, 1995.
George F. Will	"'Compassion' on Campus," *Newsweek*, May 31, 1993.

Has the Civil Rights Movement Become a "Victimhood" Competition?

Chapter Preface

While the Civil Rights Act of 1964 banned discrimination in employment on the basis of race, color, religion, or sex, subsequent legislation—for instance, the Americans with Disabilities Act of 1990 (ADA)—has extended workplace protection tó additional groups, such as the disabled. Supporters of the ADA claim that it has increased opportunities for the disabled by making workplaces more accessible to them. Detractors maintain that it has encouraged workers to invent "disabilities" in order to obtain entitlements and preferential treatment.

Jay Mathews, a *Washington Post* staff writer, is among those who applaud the ADA. He states, "The advent of the Americans with Disabilities Act, an attempt to extend new rights and opportunities to millions of people, has begun to expose the depths of the problem of hidden disabilities in the workplace." Mathews argues that protection of the rights of the disabled has encouraged a growing number of workers to ask their employers for special accommodations in the workplace. These accommodations, he contends, make them more productive workers who generate increased profits for their companies.

But Tama Starr, president of Artkraft Strauss Sign Corporation in New York City, has a different perspective on the effects of the ADA. She and numerous others are critical of the proliferation of lawsuits over rights and entitlements engendered by the legislation, believing that many of the claims are frivolous. Starr complains about the number of lawsuits charging "discrimination" that she and her company have had to defend against. She exclaims, "As an employer in the age of hyperfairness, *I'm* a victim too. Call me severely lawyer-impaired."

The proliferation of lawsuits in America has prompted many commentators, both liberal and conservative, to call for a moratorium on the creation of new rights and entitlements. Others worry that such a moratorium would delay the attainment of social justice for many disadvantaged groups. The viewpoints in the following chapter debate the effects on American society of the expansion of civil rights and of the framing of issues in terms of rights.

"What most Americans reject is the transmogrification of the civil rights movement . . . into an all-purpose movement of group victimization and special entitlements."

The Civil Rights Movement Has Become a Victimhood Competition

Richard John Neuhaus

The civil rights movement of American blacks in the 1950s and 1960s became the model for rights campaigns by women, gays, the disabled, and other minorities. In the following viewpoint, Richard John Neuhaus argues that the overstated claims for special rights made by these interest groups trivialize the worthy goals of the original movement. He contends that this competition for entitlements by "victimized" groups produces divisiveness in American society. Neuhaus is editor in chief of *First Things: A Monthly Journal of Religion and Public Life*.

As you read, consider the following questions:

1. What was the civil rights movement specifically directed at, in Neuhaus's opinion?
2. What other movements grew out of the civil rights movement in the mid-sixties, according to the author?

Richard John Neuhaus, "Hijacking the Civil Rights Movement," *First Things: A Monthly Journal of Religion and Public Life*, March 1995. Reprinted with permission.

Again the other day, one runs across an article that observes in passing, as though it is taken-for-granted knowledge, that the conservative trend in our political culture reflects Americans' rejection of the civil rights movement of the 1960s. This is, in our view, mischievous nonsense. What most Americans reject is the transmogrification of the civil rights movement, which was specifically directed at righting a great wrong in black-white relations, into an all-purpose movement of group victimization and special entitlements. This grotesque twisting of what is meant by civil rights has not been lost on some blacks. Writing in the influential black paper, *Chicago Defender*, Ray Scannell puts it this way.

> The attack on the character of Associate U.S. Supreme Court Justice Clarence Thomas by militant white feminists, in books and newspaper articles, should not be ignored by anyone concerned with the misuse of the Black American Civil Rights Movement. Media feminist activists are using allegations of personal misbehavior that are over ten years old and selective personal anecdotes to discredit the ability and judgment of a high profile professional jurist. The efforts can only be rationalized as ongoing attempts at intimidating Justice Thomas in personal behavior cases that will come before him. Character assassination aside, it is time for anyone seriously concerned with social justice to examine the damage the feminist movement has done to the Black American Civil Rights Movement. The use of administrative agency case law to license group entitlements and legal preferences has been the undoing of the movement in the post-1964 years. Equating laissez faire personal behavior as a concern for principled civil rights is a gross misinterpretation of the law. Recent sex discrimination cases resulting in large settlements, in some cases awards of multi-million dollars, to be split with aggressive trial attorneys, are the latest examples of misusing the Civil Rights Act of 1964. The increasing number of sexual misbehavior cases and the huge settlements and awards demonstrate the success of post-1964 militant feminists in co-opting the concerns of the Black American Civil Rights Movement to advance their group self-interest for private gain.

The Transformation of the Civil Rights Movement

In the mid-sixties; most of the proponents of the civil rights movement segued into the anti-Vietnam war movement, then into the more generalized counterculture, with all of its continuing sideshows of radical feminism, gay advocacy, and so forth. For many who still call themselves liberal, all these diverse and frequently contradictory movements constitute The Movement, a continuous course of progressive change. For some, it has been possible for thirty years to live in The Movement, a cognitive world impervious to both internal contradictions and challenges from the outside. Apart from the fetid backwaters of the academy, nowhere has this possibility been pressed so far as in the bureaucracies of mainline Protestantism. A friend returned from a meeting of United Methodist social justice executives who were evaluating the significance of the November 1994 election [in which Republicans won a majority of seats in the House of Representatives and the Senate for the first time in forty years] and reports that the conclusion seemed to be unanimous: The November election represented the last desperate hurrah of the white, male, racist establishment to perpetuate its control of American society.

Reprinted by permission of Chuck Asay and Creators Syndicate.

Such a reading strikes most of us as amusingly implausible, but it is important to understand that there are cognitive enclaves in which it is thought to be entirely persuasive. As Mr. Scannell and some other blacks (albeit still a minority) recognize, one real victim of this way of thinking is the legacy of the civil rights movement and the legitimate concerns of black, especially poor black, Americans. Through all the contortions of causes and ideologies that hijacked the civil rights movement, we have, after more than thirty years, moved from talking about "colored people" to talking about "people of color." It is by no means clear that this is much of an achievement, especially when "people of color" is now but one category in an endless catalogue of victimizations and entitlements. Black leaders also have much to answer for in allowing the interests of black Americans to be taken hostage by elite and well-funded organizations pushing causes unrelated to, frequently alien to, American blacks. Witness the precipitous and possibly fatal collapse of the National Association for the Advancement of Colored People. Latching on to the mantle of the civil rights movement gave these causes a measure of moral credibility for a time, but now they have brought discredit upon themselves and upon the movement to which they parasitically attached their ambitions.

This is a great shame, for the civil rights movement of, say, 1956 to 1964 was a luminous moment in American history. Martin Luther King, Jr., whatever problems people may have with his personal life or philosophy, is deservedly lifted up as a figure who helped remedy a great wrong in our national experience. It is not only blacks who are deprived when the movement that he led is exploited and trivialized by interest groups and ideologues intent upon embroiling America in a class warfare in which blacks are but one, and by no means the most important, of alleged victim classes.

"Civil rights is not about deciding who gets the spoils. It is about reclaiming our fundamental values and aspirations as a nation."

The Civil Rights Movement Is Not a Victimhood Competition

Deval L. Patrick

The rights campaigns of women, gays, the disabled, and other minorities were modeled on the civil rights movement of blacks in the 1950s and 1960s. Some critics argue that these various rights movements have become a "victimhood competition." In the following viewpoint, Deval L. Patrick argues that the struggles for rights of different groups and people strengthen rather than diminish the rights of others. He contends that the false portrayal of rights campaigners as competitors for entitlements leads to divisiveness in American society. Patrick is the U.S. assistant attorney general for civil rights.

As you read, consider the following questions:

1. What is the foremost principle on which America is founded, in the author's opinion?
2. How do many people think of civil rights, according to the author?

Excerpted from Deval L. Patrick, "Struggling for Civil Rights Now," a speech delivered on October 4, 1994, at the Town Hall Los Angeles Luncheon. Full text available in *Vital Speeches of the Day*, November 15, 1994.

Our national creed has its roots in the earliest days of the republic. In the Declaration of Independence, our founders set forth the fundamental principles for which this nation stands. Foremost among these principles is a commitment to *one* nation, indivisible—a recognition that the fate of each one of us is inextricably bound to that of each other and of society as a whole. Our common ideals tell us that we cannot progress as a society by leaving some of our people behind; we must all advance together.

The second fundamental principle of our national creed follows necessarily from the first: all people are created equal. Abraham Lincoln dedicated our nation to this proposition, and we as a people have borne faith to it ever since. It is a part of our shared American identity. History will ultimately judge us by our efforts to meet this commitment.

Affirming Civil Rights Principles

It is our faith in affirming these principles—of equality, opportunity and fair play—that makes us Americans. To be sure, we have never fully attained the high ideals to which we are dedicated. But—with a few brief exceptions—our history is a history of reaching for our ideals, of closing the gap between our reality and our ideals. Lincoln explained it well when he said our nation's founders

> meant to set up a standard maxim for free society, which should be familiar to all, and revered by all; constantly looked to, constantly labored for, and even though never perfectly attained, constantly approximated, and thereby constantly spreading and deepening its influence, and augmenting the happiness and value of life to people of all colors everywhere.

By fighting to expand opportunities, to promote equality, and to empower all people in our society, we are continuing the process Lincoln spoke of—the constant attempt to approximate our nation's great ideals, to spread and deepen their influence. Martin Luther King, Jr., was right when he said, "The arc of the moral universe is long, but it bends toward justice." All those people of perspective in all walks of American life, who work to ensure that the arc bends forward rather than backward, are engaged in a true act of patriotism.

Civil Rights Are Not a Competition

Some would have us see civil rights as a fight among competing factions for entitlements. Some would have us believe that one group's gain is another's loss, that those who want their rights vindicated are engaged in special pleading, and that civil rights is of concern to only so-called special interests. Abstract debates about colorblindness and hysterical rhetoric about quotas have been so prominent in public discourse that many people think of civil rights as simply a battleground over who gets what size slice of the pie. In such an atmosphere, is it any wonder that we see groups turning inward and refusing to invest in each other's struggles?

Expanding the Civil Rights Movement

Andrea Dworkin: The classic civil rights struggle was around the ways in which African-Americans were excluded from the body politic in the U.S. and were excluded from the experience of human dignity.

John Lewis: Right. We were visible, but invisible. And that's the way women have been treated. Blacks, African-Americans, became objects in a sense, to be used, to be abused. Women are subjected to that same status in American society. As participants in the civil rights movement, we African-Americans had to make ourselves visible. During the 1960s, there was a lot of dirt and filth under the American rug, in the cracks and in the corner—and people didn't see it. So we had to do something. By dramatizing the evil of segregation and racial discrimination, by dramatizing the denial of human dignity, we made ourselves visible and then you had the Voting Rights Act of 1965 and that type of thing. Now, as we move toward the 21st century, women have to become more visible. They have to bring the dirt out of the bedroom, out of the closet, and let people see it. So, we are no longer invisible.

Andrea Dworkin and John Lewis, interviewed by Merle Hoffman, *On the Issues*, Fall 1994.

But we *all* have a stake in the struggle for equality, opportunity and fair play. When an African-American stands up for the right to equal educational opportunity, he stands up for *all* of us. When a Latina stands up for the right to a chance to elect the candidate of her choice, she stands up for *all* of us. When a Jew stands up against those who vandalize his place of worship, he stands up for *all* of us. And when a person with a hearing impairment stands up for access to 911 emergency services, she stands up for *all* of us. For civil rights is not about deciding who gets the spoils. It is about reclaiming our fundamental values and aspirations as a nation.

It *is* a struggle. It is often hard work. But we must resist this tendency towards the dissolution of our society into mutually isolated and mutually distrustful groups. For if we don't, we will surely perish. And the nation our forebears imagined—and have entrusted now to us—will never come to pass. We must stick together in this struggle: not simply because it is politically correct, but because it is morally correct.

This is a defining point in history: our young people are increasingly alienated from civic society, and too many of the rest of us have let cynicism and selfishness define our lives. But I believe in America still. President Bill Clinton fervently does. And so must you. Diverse a people as we are and have always been—we are still *one* nation, *one* people, with *one* common destiny. And each of us is diminished when any one—on account of a happenstance of birth or chance—experiences anything less than the full measure of his or her dignity and privilege as a human being and an American. So, let us recapture our perspective, set aside our hysterics, and reclaim the American conscience. Destiny demands of us no less.

"The incessant issuance of new rights . . . causes a massive inflation of rights that devalues their moral claims."

Overemphasizing Civil Rights Undermines Civic Responsibility

Amitai Etzioni

Communitarians believe that the source of America's decline of civic responsibility lies in an excessive emphasis on civil rights. In the following viewpoint, Amitai Etzioni argues that to restore a sense of community responsibility, Americans should place a moratorium on the creation of new rights and begin to focus more attention on public safety and community. Etzioni is a founder of the Communitarian Network, the editor of the quarterly communitarian journal the *Responsive Community*, and author of *The Spirit of Community: Rights, Responsibilities, and the Communitarian Agenda*, from which this viewpoint is excerpted.

As you read, consider the following questions:

1. According to John Leo, quoted by the author, how does rights talk polarize debate?
2. What example does Etzioni give of a responsibility that does not entail a right?
3. What is the best way to curb authoritarianism and right-wing tendencies, in the author's opinion?

Excerpted from *The Spirit of Community: Rights, Responsibilities, and the Communitarian Agenda* by Amitai Etzioni (New York: Crown, 1993); ©1993 by Amitai Etzioni. Reprinted by permission of the author.

From time to time there's a finding of social science that may by itself be of limited importance but illuminates a major conundrum: A 1983 study has shown that young Americans expect to be tried before a jury of their peers but are rather reluctant to serve on one. This paradox highlights a major aspect of contemporary American civic culture: a strong sense of entitlement—that is, a demand that the community provide more services and strongly uphold rights—coupled with a rather weak sense of obligation to the local and national community. Thus, most Americans applauded the show of force in Grenada (in 1983), Panama (in 1989–1990), and in the Persian Gulf (in 1991), but many were reluctant to serve in the armed forces or see their sons and daughters called up.

First prize for capturing this anticommunitarian outlook should be awarded to a member of a television audience who exclaimed during a show on the savings and loan mess, "The taxpayers should not have to pay for this; the government should," as if there really were an Uncle Sam who could pick up the tab for us all.

The Imbalance of Rights and Responsibilities

A 1989 study by People for the American Way notes:

> Young people have learned only half of America's story. Consistent with the priority they place on personal happiness, young people reveal notions of America's unique character that emphasize freedom and license almost to the complete exclusion of service or participation. Although they clearly appreciate the democratic freedoms that, in their view, make theirs the "best country in the world to live in," they fail to perceive a need to reciprocate by exercising the duties and responsibilities of good citizenship.

Only one out of eight (12 percent) of the respondents felt that voting was part of what makes a good citizen. When asked what was special about the United States, young people responded: "Individualism and the fact that it is a democracy and you can do whatever you want." And: "We really don't have any limits."

The imbalance between rights and responsibilities has existed for a long time. Indeed, some argue that it is a basic trait of the American character. However, America's leaders have exacerbated this tendency in recent years. In 1961 President John F. Kennedy could still stir the nation when he stated: "Ask not what your country can do for you. Ask what you can do for your country." But Presidents Ronald Reagan and George Bush, backed up by some Democrats in Congress, proposed a much less onerous course: they suggested that ever-increasing economic growth would pay for government services, and taxpayers would be expected to shell out less—implying that Americans could have their cake and eat it, too. . . .

Correcting the current imbalance between rights and responsibilities requires a four-point agenda: a moratorium on the minting of most, if not all, new rights; reestablishing the link between rights and responsibilities; recognizing that some responsibilities do not entail rights; and, most carefully, adjusting some rights to the changed circumstances. These pivotal points deserve some elaboration.

A Moratorium

We should, for a transition period of, say, the next decade, put a tight lid on the manufacturing of new rights. The incessant issuance of new rights, like the wholesale printing of currency, causes a massive inflation of rights that devalues their moral claims.

When asked whether certain things are "a privilege that a person should have to earn, or a right to which he is entitled as a citizen," most Americans (81 percent) considered health care a right (versus 16 percent who said it was a privilege). Two-thirds (66 percent) considered adequate housing a right (as opposed to 31 percent who called it a privilege). Indeed, why not? Until one asks, as there are no free lunches, who will pay for unlimited health care and adequate housing for all? The champions of rights are often quite mum on this question, which if left unanswered makes the claim for a right a rather empty gesture. . . .

Once, rights were very solemn moral/legal claims, ensconced in the Constitution and treated with much reverence. We all lose if the publicity department of every special interest can claim that someone's rights are violated every time they don't get all they want. Suspending for a while the minting of new rights, unless there are unusually compelling reasons to proceed, will serve to restore the special moral standing and suasion of rights.

We need to remind one another that *each newly minted right generates a claim on someone.* In effect, new rights often arouse or play upon feelings of guilt in others. There is a limited amount of guilt, however, that one can lay upon other people before they balk. Unless we want to generate a universal backlash against rights, we need to curb rights inflation and protect the currency of rights from being further devalued.

Conflicting Rights Claims

Moreover, the expression of ever more wants, many quite legitimate, in the language of rights makes it difficult to achieve compromises and to reach consensus, processes that lie at the heart of democracy. A society that is studded with groups of true believers and special-interest groups, each brimming with rights, inevitably turns into a society overburdened with conflicts. Columnist John Leo of *U.S. News & World Report* declares: "Rights talk polarizes debate; it tends to suppress moral discussion and consensus building. Once an agenda is introduced as a 'right,' sensible discussion and moderate positions tend to disappear."

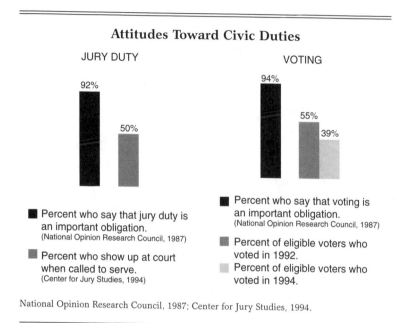

Attitudes Toward Civic Duties

JURY DUTY

VOTING

■ Percent who say that jury duty is an important obligation.
(National Opinion Research Council, 1987)

■ Percent who show up at court when called to serve.
(Center for Jury Studies, 1994)

■ Percent who say that voting is an important obligation.
(National Opinion Research Council, 1987)

■ Percent of eligible voters who voted in 1992.

■ Percent of eligible voters who voted in 1994.

National Opinion Research Council, 1987; Center for Jury Studies, 1994.

Even if lawyers and judges realize among themselves that individual rights are limited by the rights of others and the needs of the community, as the language of rights penetrates into everyday discourse, the discourse becomes impoverished and confrontational. It is one thing to claim that you and I have different interests and see if we can work out a compromise; or, better yet, that we both recognize the merit or virtue of a common cause, say, a cleaner environment. The moment, however, that I claim a *right* to the same piece of land or property or public space as you, we start to view one another like the Catholics and Protestants in Northern Ireland or the Palestinians and Israelis in the Middle East.

A return to a language of social virtues, interests, and, above all, social responsibilities will reduce contentiousness and enhance social cooperation.

People treat rights-based arguments, unlike many others, as "trump cards" that neutralize all other positions. Cass R. Sunstein, professor of jurisprudence at the University of Chicago,

65

put it well when he pointed out that rights can "be conclusions masquerading as reasons." For example, he writes, those who defend even the most extreme kinds of what he labels violent pornography state that it is a form of free speech, period. Sunstein suggests that perhaps a person is entitled to this particularly abusive form of speech. But, he argues, an individual's entitlement should be established in detailed argumentation that would weigh the right at issue against the rights of those who are hurt by the given act, rather than simply asserting that it is a right, as if its evocation closed off all debate.

Individual Rights and Harming Others

Mary Ann Glendon, a Harvard Law professor and leading Communitarian, shows that we treat many rights the way we treat property, which we tend to view as intrinsically "ours" and which we are therefore free to do with as we wish. Actually, we readily accept that there are many things we may not do with things we own, such as burning leaves, which may endanger others, or playing the stereo loud enough to be heard five blocks away. To put it differently, we all know on one level that our liberties are limited by those of others and that we can do what we want only *as long as we do not harm others*. Rights talk, however, pushes us to disregard this crucial qualification, the concern for one another and for the community. Soon "I can do what I want as long as I do not hurt others" becomes "I can do what I want, because I have a right to do it."

A telling case in point is the opposition to seat belts and motorcycle helmets. Libertarians have long argued adamantly that the government should not require people to use these safety devices. They blocked the introduction of seat belt and motorcycle helmet laws in many jurisdictions and ensured the repeal of such regulations in several localities where they had been in place. The main libertarian argument is that people have a right to do with their lives what they wish, including endangering them. People are said to be the best judges of what is good for them, because they will have to live with the consequences of their acts. Therefore we should treat people as adults and not as children, without paternalism. (Some libertarians apply the same idea to the use of narcotics.)

Reckless individuals, however, do not absorb many of the consequences of their acts. Drivers without seat belts are more likely than those wearing belts to lose control of their cars in an accident and hurtle into others. They are also more likely to die and leave their children for society to attend to and pick up the pieces. And, of course, they draw on our community resources, from ambulance services to hospitals, when they are involved in accidents, for which they pay at best a fraction of the cost. To insist that people drive safely and responsibly is hence a concern for the needs of others and the community; there is no individual right that automatically trumps these considerations. . . .

Rights Presume Responsibilities

Claiming rights without assuming responsibilities is unethical and illogical. Mary Ann Glendon puts it well: "Buried deep in our rights dialect," she writes, "is an unexpressed premise that we roam at large in a land of strangers, where we presumptively have no obligations toward others except to avoid the active infliction of harm." She notes in her book *Rights Talk:*

> Try, for example, to find in the familiar language of our Declaration of Independence or Bill of Rights anything comparable to the statements in the Universal Declaration of Human Rights that "everyone has duties to the community," and that everyone's rights and freedoms are subject to limitations "for the purposes of securing due recognition and respect for the rights and freedoms of others and of meeting the just requirements of morality, public order and the general welfare in a democratic society."

The Constitution, while not nearly as explicit on obligations to the community as the other documents cited, does open with the quest "to form a more perfect Union" and speaks of the need to "promote the general welfare" for that purpose.

To take and not to give is an amoral, self-centered predisposition that ultimately no society can tolerate. To revisit the finding that many try to evade serving on a jury, which, they claim, they have a right to be served by, is egotistical, indecent, and in the long run impractical. Hence, *those most concerned about rights ought to be the first ones to argue for the resumption of responsibilities.* One presumes the other. Much of the discussion about the conditions under which moral commitments can be strengthened in the family, schools, and in communities speaks directly to the shoring up of our responsibilities. Indeed, many of our core values entail concern for others and the commons we share. As we restore the moral voice of communities (and the web of social bonds, the Communitarian nexus, that enables us to speak as a community), we shall see, we will also be more able to encourage one another to live up to our social responsibilities.

Responsibilities Without Rights

Although it is difficult to imagine rights without corollary responsibilities, we must recognize that we have some duties that lay moral claims on us from which we derive no immediate benefit or even long-term payoff. Our commitment to a shared future, especially our responsibility to the environment, is a case in point. We are to care for the environment not only or even mainly for our own sakes (although we may desire some assurance of potable water, breathable air, and protection from frying because the ozone layer is thinning out). We have a moral commitment to leave for future generations a livable environment, even perhaps a better one than the one we inherited, certainly not one that has been further depleted. *The same observations hold true for our responsibility to our moral, social, and political environment.*

Careful Adjustments

Finally, some areas in which legal rights have been interpreted in ways that hobble public safety and health are to be reinterpreted. Thus, the Fourth Amendment outlaws *unreasonable* searches and seizures. The question of what is deemed reasonable versus unreasonable is subject to change over time. In several areas of public life, the times now call for a modest increase in what we can reasonably be asked to do for the sake of the community, for public safety and public health.

Radical Individualists, such as libertarians and the American Civil Liberties Union (ACLU), have effectively blocked many steps to increase public safety and health. Among the measures they systematically oppose are sobriety checkpoints (which can play an important role in reducing slaughter on the highways), *all* drug testing (even of those who have the lives of others directly in their control), and limiting the flood of private money into the pockets, drawers, and war chests of local and national elected representatives.

Having presented this fourth part of the Communitarian agenda before scores of groups, my colleagues and I have learned that this element of balancing rights and responsibilities is the most controversial. . . . Such adjustments can be made without opening the floodgates to a police state or excessive intrusion by public health departments. On the contrary, *the best way to curb authoritarianism and right-wing tendencies is to stop the anarchic drift by introducing carefully calibrated responses to urgent and legitimate public concerns* about safety and the control of epidemics.

"[Communitarians] consistently fail to appreciate the positive contributions of the modern 'rights revolution' in creating a more meaningful community in this country."

Overemphasizing Civic Responsibility Undermines Civil Rights

Samuel Walker

Members of the communitarian movement have called for a moratorium on the proliferation of new rights and for the renewal of an emphasis on civic responsibility. In the following viewpoint, Samuel Walker criticizes the platform of the communitarian movement. He argues that many of the communitarians' prescriptions for social problems are the same as those advocated by traditional civil libertarians, whom communitarians criticize. He contends that communitarians undervalue the contributions that the civil rights movement has made to American society. Walker is a professor of criminal justice at the University of Nebraska at Omaha and is a member of the board of directors of the American Civil Liberties Union.

As you read, consider the following questions:

1. What criticism of the communitarian position on families and social services does Walker offer?
2. In Walker's opinion, what function does strident and absolutist rhetoric serve?

Excerpted from Samuel Walker, "The Communitarian Cop-Out." Reprinted with permission from the *National Civic Review*, Summer 1993, pp. 246–53; ©1993 National Civic League Press. All rights reserved.

It is time to declare a "moratorium" on the "manufacturing of new rights"; time to match individual rights with an equal concern with "social responsibilities." So argues Amitai Etzioni, founder and leader of the communitarian movement. Communitarianism has emerged as a new force in American political and intellectual life. President Clinton and Vice President Gore have reportedly said that communitarianism expresses their values. Gore, moreover, attended the first communitarian "teach-in" on Capitol Hill in late 1990, along with such odd bedfellows as Senators Daniel Moynihan and Alan Simpson. With a journal [The Responsive Community], an official platform, a book by Etzioni [The Spirit of Community], and the Clinton-Gore connection, communitarianism has received an enormous amount of attention.

The Emergence of Communitarianism

What is communitarianism? According to the official platform it seeks to restore a "moral voice" to our political dialogue, a concern for "the social dimensions of human existence." This includes strengthening the family, restoring moral education to the public school curriculum, and rebuilding communities.

The source of our current ills, communitarians argue, is society's excessive concern with rights. Our "hyperindividualism," they say, has fostered a self-centered outlook that is heedless of the common interest. Mary Ann Glendon, professor of law at Harvard and co-drafter of the communitarian platform, argues that our language of rights is "morally incomplete," with no concern for our responsibility to others. Etzioni calls for a new sense of "we-ness." The self-centered ethos of today undermines the family and leads to rampant divorce and neglect of children, he says. Excessive concern for Fourth Amendment rights harms public safety, for example, by preventing the police from conducting random stops for drunk drivers. The pursuit of group rights has balkanized American society into hostile subcommunities, obliterating any sense of a common culture. Glendon argues that the "strident" and "absolutist" quality of our rights rhetoric precludes mutual understanding and compromise.

The communitarians offer a number of specific remedies for all this. In addition to a "moratorium" on new rights, we should discourage divorce, grant police expanded powers and restore "moral education" to the public school curriculum. Etzioni's quick to assure us that this does not mean "religious indoctrination," or a fundamentalist takeover of the schools. A mainstream liberal, Etzioni argues that the best way to combat the far right is to end the anarchy that our obsession with rights has brought upon us.

The communitarians are particularly disturbed about the degeneration of American politics: the dominance of simplistic "sound bites," the enormous power of special interest groups, and the increasing cynicism and apathy of the electorate. They propose limits on political campaign contributions and call for a new commitment to the "public interest," in the spirit of pre–World War I Progressivism.

Communitarianism has attracted so much attention so quickly in large part because it expresses the concerns of a broad segment of the American people. Conservatives and liberals alike are deeply alarmed over crime and the crisis of the family. Many people are increasingly disturbed over the rise of group consciousness, as represented by the demands for Afro-centric education. Liberal historian Arthur Schlesinger, Jr. deplores this trend in his latest book, pointedly entitled *The Disuniting of America*. Art critic Robert Hughes incorporates many of the same objections to group consciousness in his best-seller, *Culture of Complaint*. Conservatives have been waging a holy war on the growth of rights for twenty-five years. Communitarianism's appeal lies in linking an unease over rights with a wider range of issues and a seemingly attractive call for a new moral vision in politics and social policy.

The Lack of a Program

Beyond the slogans, what do the communitarians propose? Do they point us in the direction of a revitalized politics and a healthier society? The short answer is no. Despite the high-sounding rhetoric, communitarians do not offer a program likely to build a stronger sense of community in America. First, many of their proposals are without any real substance. Second, they consistently refuse to challenge established economic orthodoxy, even though their arguments inescapably point in that direction. Third, a few of their ideas represent a drastic extension of coercive government intervention in private lives, all in the name of community. Fourth, they consistently fail to appreciate the positive contributions of the modern "rights revolution" in creating a more meaningful community in this country. The communitarian attack on rights, wittingly or unwittingly, serves the right-wing agenda.

The question of divorce, which is central to their concern about the family, illustrates the intellectual emptiness of the communitarian program. They don't like divorce, but can't bring themselves to outlaw it, or even make it more difficult to obtain. Instead they exhort us to "discourage" it (unless otherwise noted, all references to communitarian policies are taken from their official platform). This is a nice idea but one unlikely to have any effect on the divorce rate. Many of their other proposals are little more than exhortations to "be nice" and "do good."

To help families, the communitarians call for a comprehensive

program of family-oriented social services: family leave programs, workplace child care facilities, and so on. Such programs
are long overdue in this country, but they are not inconsistent
with either a reinvigorated liberalism or the continued pursuit
of rights. There is nothing unique to communitarianism here.
More serious is the fact that they do not attack the real culprits
behind our scandalously inadequate social service system: the
conservative political movement that for generations has attacked "big government," "government spending" and "social-
ized medicine." Instead, they argue that the problem is too
much concern with rights, as if it is all the fault of the National
Association for the Advancement of Colored People (NAACP),
the American Civil Liberties Union (ACLU), the National Organization for Women (NOW), and other rights groups.

Voluntary vs. Legal Restraint

The communitarian position on hate speech dramatizes its intellectual shortcomings. Communitarians argue that while we
may have a legal right to call someone an offensive name, we
should not exercise that right: Right does not mean "rightness."
Voluntary restraint in the name of the common good is one of
the central tenets of communitarianism.

This is a nice idea, but not much help in a society torn by
racial and religious conflict. Of course we should not call people
names. I doubt that anyone reading this piece ever does. But a
lot of other people do. Telling a skinhead to "be nice" isn't likely
to curb expressions of hate. In the end, the communitarian platform affirms the importance of protecting free speech. Instead
of attempting to outlaw hate speech, the communitarian platform advises, we should respond to racist incidents through
nonlegal steps, such as campus teach-ins on racism.

The communitarian hate speech policy is, in fact, identical to
the ACLU's policy. This is a bit odd, because on most issues, the
communitarians use the ACLU as their favorite whipping boy.
The ACLU's "radical individualism" is the cause of all our problems, they say. Yet, if the ACLU's absolutist approach is wrong on
the Fourth, Eighth, and Fourteenth Amendments, why is it right
on the First Amendment? The communitarians never provide a
good explanation of how and when we should "balance" rights.

Defining Acceptable Limits on Rights

Mary Ann Glendon strongly recommends the balancing and
communal ethos expressed in most international human rights
declarations. Article 19 of the International Covenant on Civil
and Political Rights (1966), for example, holds that the rights of
free speech, equality, due process, and others can be limited in
the interest of protecting "the rights and reputations of others,"

"national security," "public order," or "public morality." She seems blithely unaware that these have been the traditional rationales for suppressing civil liberties in the United States. Critics of the government were jailed during World War I in the name of national security; *Ulysses* by James Joyce and many other works of art were banned to protect public morality; civil rights demonstrators were arrested for violating public order; and so on. Glendon, the most articulate of all the leading communitarians, never explains the exact scope of acceptable limitations on rights.

Why the ACLU Defends Rights

Cathy Young: Are there areas in which exercising one fundamental right precludes exercising others? . . .

Nadine Strossen: It's common to say that we have to choose between freedom of speech or equality, that if you really care about equality you can't possibly be devoted to the First Amendment. I absolutely reject that as a philosophical matter and as a practical matter. . . .

I think there may be particular situations at the margins where rights might come into conflict. . . . But in the vast, vast, vast majority of cases, I think those rights are mutually reinforcing. It's that understanding that has led the ACLU from its beginning to attempt to consistently defend all fundamental rights for all people precisely because they are indivisible. If the government is given the power to threaten one right for one person, it can and will use that power to erode other rights for other people.

Nadine Strossen, interviewed by Cathy Young, *Reason*, October 1994.

The communitarian proposal to restore the "moral education" role of the public schools is vague and empty. They assure us that it does not mean "religious indoctrination." They do not support the agenda of Christian fundamentalists. Historically, however, local majorities have used the public schools as instruments for promoting *their* religious views, which is to say, their view of community values. The communitarian platform says they are "not majoritarians," but they do not explain what the majority can and cannot do with the public school curriculum.

The communitarian idea of moral education involves inculcating the "shared values" of America: the dignity of all people, tolerance, and nondiscrimination. These happen to be very secular values that form the core values of the ACLU's vision of civil liberties. Once again, the communitarians seek to score points by bashing libertarianism, but end up endorsing its basic values. Communitarians advise us to teach tolerance and equality, but they attack the rights groups that have fought for these values. . . .

The Success of the Rights Revolution

Communitarians argue that the so-called rights revolution—all this clamoring for "my rights" and "our rights"—has destroyed community in America. To the contrary: The rights revolution has created a more meaningful community in America. It also goes without saying that membership is the essential condition of community. The communitarians admit, of course, that the civil rights movement was one of the epic events of recent history. From a community perspective, the end of jim crow and disenfranchisement removed the formal barriers to membership in the community.

Communitarians fail to appreciate how the various rights movements that have followed and been inspired by the original civil rights movement have secured a greater measure of membership and participation for other groups. The current struggle over gay and lesbian rights is the most obvious example. To secure formal rights for gay and lesbian people is to acknowledge that they are legitimate members of the American community. Why, then, do the communitarians want us to lower our voices about rights? Do they honestly believe that we have achieved full equality for all people? . . .

The First Amendment rights of speech, press and assembly have historically been the principal guardians of the right of membership: the right to speak and to be heard. Even to assert one's First Amendment rights is to become a participating member. When young African-Americans sat-in and demonstrated in the Deep South during the early 1960s they transformed the politics of their time—that is, they became participating members of the community by those acts alone. Segregationists understood this very well. The mass arrest of demonstrators was designed to stop that participation and maintain African-Americans as less-than-full members.

In an earlier era, the First Amendment struggles surrounding birth control advocate Margaret Sanger ultimately involved the question of membership. When Boston Mayor James Curley banned Sanger from speaking, he knew full well that information about contraception was directly related to women controlling their own bodies and ending their subordination. Censorship served patriarchy. And by the same token, the First Amendment served the cause of women's equality.

Current censorship controversies over gay and lesbian issues follow the same pattern. The fundamentalists and homophobes understand perfectly well that even to discuss same-sex relationships is to confer legitimacy on them—and to say that gays and lesbians are entitled to the same respect as all members of the community.

Shutting Groups Up

By suggesting that we all cool our rhetoric about rights, communitarians serve the conservative agenda. How would the public at-large know that a group was the victim of discrimination unless that group asserted its claim to rights? To tell people to lower their voices is a polite way of telling them to sit down and shut up—in short, don't disturb the status quo.

Mary Ann Glendon's complaints about the "strident" and "absolutist" quality of rights rhetoric is particularly puzzling. If fundamental moral issues are involved, shouldn't people express themselves in the strongest terms? Would she have counselled the abolitionists to moderate their criticisms of slavery?

Strident and absolutist rhetoric actually serves a very important educational function. When I was in college thirty years ago I never thought about when life begins, even though it is obviously a profoundly important question. Nor did I think about a right to privacy, its scope, and whether the Constitution guarantees it. I think about these matters all the time now, because the abortion controversy has forced me to. The strident and absolutist rhetoric of the pro-lifers has forced me to examine my abortion rights position, to make sure that it is really the right position. In the same fashion, nearly everyone in this country has been forced to think about these and other issues.

In the end, that is the function of rights advocacy. The vigorous pursuit of rights makes us think—think about things we never thought of before, or would prefer not to think about. That advocacy is often strident, at times obnoxious, sometimes even offensive. The uncompromising pursuit of rights, however, is central to the process of public debate that is the essential feature of a living and ever-changing democratic community. When they ask us to tone down our rhetoric and to be less demanding about rights, communitarians are really asking us to stop thinking, to lower our standards for society, and to halt the process of social change.

"Everyone else is getting run over as those with rights try to get to where they want."

The Disabled Rights Movement Is Counterproductive

Philip K. Howard

The Americans with Disabilities Act (ADA) was enacted in 1990 to prevent discrimination against the disabled. In the following viewpoint, Philip K. Howard argues that the ADA and similar statutes have provided unassailable rights to the disabled and imposed unfair costs on everyone else in society, including other disadvantaged groups. He contends that government should balance the rights of different groups and spread the costs evenly. Howard is a business lawyer and author of *The Death of Common Sense: How Law Is Suffocating America*, from which this viewpoint is excerpted.

As you read, consider the following questions:

1. Prior to the past few decades what were rights synonymous with, according to Howard?
2. How are rights for the disabled particularly paradoxical, in the author's opinion?
3. According to the author, how many Americans are supposedly protected by the ADA?

Finding a public bathroom in New York City is not easy. Most subway toilets were closed down years ago because of vandalism and crime. Museums require people to pay admission. Restaurant bathrooms are restricted to patrons' use. As public toilets became scarce, the nooks and crannies around the city began to exude the malodorous costs of this shortage. "No one needed to be told that this was a serious problem," observed Joan Davidson, a director of a private foundation, the J.M. Kaplan Fund.

Ms. Davidson was nonetheless surprised at the outpouring of enthusiasm when, in 1991, the Kaplan Fund put forward a modest proposal to finance a test of six sidewalk toilet kiosks in different sections of the city. The coin-operated toilets would be imported from Paris, where the municipal government provides them for the convenience of residents and tourists. Perfected over years of experience in Paris, these facilities were almost too good to be true. They clean themselves with a shower of water and disinfectant after each use. The doors open automatically after fifteen minutes so they cannot be used as a place to spend the night. They are small, only five feet in diameter, which means that New York's crowded sidewalks would not be blocked. And while the City of Paris rents them, they would cost budget-strapped New York nothing: Advertising panels would be added on the outside to pay the freight. City Hall was ready to move. The six-month test, in sites from Harlem down to City Hall, would show whether they would work in New York.

Equal Access to Public Toilets

Then came the glitch. Wheelchairs couldn't fit inside them. New York's antidiscrimination law provides that it is illegal to "withhold or deny" from the disabled any access to "public accommodation." Ann Emerman, the head of the Mayor's Office of the Disabled, characterized the sidewalk toilet proposal as "discrimination in its purest form." When the city's chief lawyer, Victor Kovner, whose credentials as a champion of liberal causes stretch back thirty years, sought a legislative amendment to permit the six-month test, another lobbyist for the disabled accused him of "conspiring to violate the law." Never mind that he was seeking to amend the law through the democratic process.

Suggestions that disabled-accessible bathrooms might be provided in nearby buildings or restaurants were dismissed out-of-hand: "The law requires that everyone go to the bathroom in exactly the same place." When someone had the nerve, at a public forum, to ask how many wheelchair users there might be compared with other citizens who might benefit (including blind and deaf citizens), the questioner was hooted down for asking a politically incorrect question. At stake, at least for the disabled, were their "rights." When you have a right to something, it doesn't matter what anyone thinks or whether you are, in fact, reasonable. . . .

The Language of Rights

Making trade-offs in situations like this is much of what government does: Almost every government act, whether allocating use of public property, creating new programs, or granting subsidies, benefits one group more than another, and usually at the expense of everyone else. Most people expect their elected and appointed leaders to balance the pros and cons and make decisions in the public interest. The government of New York, however, lacked this power, because it had passed an innocuous-sounding law that created "rights" elevating the interests of any disabled person over any other public purpose.

Rights, almost no one needs to be told, are all around us. The language of rights is used everywhere in modern America—not only in public life, but in the workplace, in school, in welfare offices, in health care. There are rights for children and the elderly; the disabled; the mentally disabled; workers under twenty-five and over forty; alcoholics and the addicted; the homeless; spotted owls and snail darters.

Rights are considered as American as apple pie. This is a country where citizens have *rights*. The Bill of Rights is the best-known part of the Constitution: Government can't tell us what to say, and can't take away our "life, liberty or property" except by due process. Rights are basic. Until the last few decades, however, rights were not something to shout about. They were the bedrock of our society, something we would give our lives to defend, but not something people thought much about as they made it through each day. Rights were synonymous with freedom, protection against being ordered around by government or others.

The New Role of Rights

Rights have taken on a new role in America. Whenever there is a perceived injustice, new rights are created to help the victims. These rights are different: While the rights-bearers may see them as "protection," they don't protect so much as provide. These rights are intended as a new, and often invisible, form of subsidy. They are provided at everyone else's expense, but the amount of the check is left blank. For example, in New York, the unintended consequence of giving the disabled the "right" to do everything in the same way was the imposition of a de facto prohibition of sidewalk toilets.

Handing out rights like land grants has become the preferred method of staking out a place for those who feel disadvantaged.

Lawmakers and courts, confronted with evidence of past abuses, scramble over each other to define and take credit for handing out new rights. When refused entry to a movie because his two-year-old son might disturb the other patrons, Rolando Acosta, then deputy commissioner of New York City's Human Rights Commission, had an easy fix; the commission ruled that banning children was age discrimination. In 1993, a judge in Rhode Island found rights for obese employees. Mari Matsuda, a feminist legal scholar, has advocated rights for those who are discriminated against on account of unusual accents—people who talk differently would be able to sue if they feel their accent is being held against them. In 1990, the federal government enacted a comprehensive disabled law, the Americans with Disabilities Act (known as the ADA), to serve similar purposes as New York's. "Let the shameful wall of exclusion finally come tumbling down," said President George Bush on the South Lawn of the White House upon signing the bill. The law had passed with virtually no opposition. After all, rights cost little or nothing out of the budget. It's only a matter of being fair. Or so we think.

The Disabilities Act's Absurdities

Gilbert Casellas, chairman of the Equal Employment Opportunity Commission, declared in May 1995 that most of the tens of thousands of lawsuits and complaints filed under the Americans with Disabilities Act have merit. The EEOC, the lead federal agency in setting ADA policy, is desperately trying to shore up the law's public image. Unfortunately, the act is producing even more absurd results than most Washington policy makers realize. . . .

[For instance:] A motorist who was ticketed by a Topeka, Kansas, police officer for not wearing a seat belt claimed that he could not wear the belt because of his claustrophobia and sued the city for violating the ADA. . . .

A government clerk in Howard County, Maryland, was fired after repeated rude outbursts and loud denunciations of her supervisors. She claimed in a lawsuit that the firing violated her civil rights because she was a manic depressive and that the employer was obliged to strip her job of all its inherent stress.

James Bovard, *Wall Street Journal*, June 22, 1995.

Rights, however, leave no room for balance, or for looking at it from everybody's point of view as well. Rights, as the legal philosopher Ronald Dworkin has noted, are a trump card. Rights give open-ended power to one group, and it comes out of everybody else's hide. What about the three hundred other moviegoers when the two-year-old starts crying or demanding candy in a loud voice? Too bad; we gave children a right. Rights cede control to those least likely to use them wisely, usually partisans like disabled activists who have devoted their lives to remedying their own injustices. Government, for all its flaws, at least has interest in a balanced result.

This abdication has led to an inverted feudalism in which the rights-bearer, by assertion of legal and moral superiority, lords it over everyone else. Rights-bearers do warfare independent of the constraints of democracy: *Give Us Our Rights.* We cringe, lacking even a vocabulary to respond.

It was only three decades ago that John F. Kennedy stirred the nation when, in his inaugural address, he said, "Ask not what your country can do for you, but what you can do for your country." Thirty years later, we have disintegrated into factions preoccupied only with our due, not what we can do. . . .

Rights in Conflict

Handing out rights does not resolve conflict. It aggravates it. "Filing complaints is the keystone of the ADA," said one advocate for the disabled. To another, passage of the law is a call to "man the barricades." But against whom? The disabled lobby is waging warfare against every other citizen.

The fight for rights becomes obsessive, like a religious conviction. One former construction worker in Rhode Island, Gregory Solas, who has been in a wheelchair since an accident in 1986, has filed over two thousand complaints under disabled laws. He has single-handedly forced Rhode Island schools to spend millions of dollars to replace doorknobs with levers, to lower light switches and fire alarms, and to reconfigure showers. He once filed a claim when a father-daughter dance was held in a building that did not have a wheelchair ramp; the school was required to move the dance. Everyone else's enjoyment was of no moment compared to the price of being helped up a few steps. Mr. Solas is on a crusade, wielding his new rights like a sword while everyone else—the common good—is defenseless. Even the elected leaders of Rhode Island have no power.

Gifted students, in contrast to disabled children, receive virtually no support or attention from America's school systems; about two cents out of every hundred dollars is allocated to programs for them. According to a recent report by the U.S. Department of Education, gifted students languish in classrooms bored stiff, doing their work left-handed, having mastered over half the curriculum before the school year begins. Nothing is done to nurture their skills or groom them to be future leaders of education, business, or government.

The ratio of funding of special education programs to gifted programs is about eleven dollars to one cent. I doubt that many legislators or officials think this balance makes sense. But Congress took away everyone's power to balance the competing needs. As columnist Anna Quindlen has observed, it's "Just dumb": We have built an educational system "obsessed with its potential failures to the detriment of its potential successes."

The Problem with Absolute Rights

The virtue of rights, at least to the advocates, is that they are absolute. What's a little inefficiency when there is complete justice for me? Absolutes sound good, but generally leave behind a landscape of paradoxes and bruised victims.

Rights for the disabled are particularly paradoxical, because what benefits a person with one disability may harm someone with another disability. Low drinking fountains and telephones are harder to use for the elderly or those with bad backs. High toilets make transfer easier from a wheelchair, but make bowel movements harder for everyone else, especially the elderly. Curb cuts are more dangerous for the blind, who have more difficulty knowing when they have reached the end of the block. Ramps are essential for wheelchairs but are sometimes slippery and dangerous for the frail. Warning bumps at the edge of a train platform are good for the blind but bad for those in wheelchairs. When confronted by a dwarf complaining that certain of the changes for the disabled made his life miserable, the director of New York's Office for the Disabled is reported to have said, "You can't please everybody." Exactly. So why is it appropriate to handle these issues as a "right"?

Rights are a kind of wealth and, like other forms of wealth, attract hangers-on. Anyone who wants something looks around to see if it fits within the orbit of some right. In recent years the number of disabled children has grown, not very mysteriously, as parents have learned that characterizing a problem as a "learning disability" carries with it special treatment. Soon, as with the proliferation of categories of citizens protected against discrimination, perhaps a majority of children will lay claim to a disability. Gifted children could claim boredom as their own special handicap. . . .

The Americans with Disabilities Act supposedly protects 43 million Americans. The overwhelming preponderance of the ADA regulations, however, and virtually all cost and conflict, relate to wheelchair users. But there are not 43 million people in wheelchairs. There are not 10 percent of that number of people in wheelchairs. It turns out, in a number that seems to have been actively suppressed (I could find it nowhere in the extensive legislative history), that not 2 percent of the disabled are in

81

wheelchairs, and many of those are confined to nursing homes. Billions are being spent to make every nook and cranny of every facility in America wheelchair-accessible (for example, by tearing down and rebuilding showers), when children die of malnutrition and finish almost dead last in math.

"It's Their Right"

Zealots, we learn time and again, always push their "right" to its absolute limit and beyond. They go as fast as they can, the rest of us be damned. "The law is the law," Mr. Solas says: "If I could, I would make them stand at a chalkboard and write, 'I will not discriminate.'" Their mission becomes an obsession, their appetite never quelled. Faster and faster. It's their right.

But we all live here together. Society needs red lights as well as green lights. Government—whether Congress or local school boards—must continually perform the role of letting one group go so far and then allowing others to go. Rights provide a perpetual green light. That means everyone else is getting run over as those with rights try to get to where they want.

The injuries are mounting, and Americans are building up a reservoir of hatred.

> *"We must reconstruct the social world to better accommodate the range of abilities of those who inhabit it."*

The Disabled Rights Movement Is Beneficial

David Wasserman

The Americans with Disabilities Act (ADA), modeled on the 1960s civil rights legislation that banned discrimination against women and minorities, was enacted in 1990 to ensure access for the disabled to public and private facilities. In the following viewpoint, David Wasserman argues that although the ADA is a major step, the disabled need more than antidiscrimination legislation; they need special structural accommodation (such as wheelchair ramps) to guarantee their right of access. Wasserman further argues that society should bear the monetary costs of this accommodation. Wasserman is a criminal defense lawyer and a research scholar at the Institute for Philosophy and Public Policy.

As you read, consider the following questions:

1. What functions does the ADA's antidiscrimination framework serve, according to Wasserman?
2. According to Jacobus tenBroek, cited by the author, what is required to ensure the rights of the disabled?
3. What does the Education for All Handicapped Children Act mandate, according to the author?

David Wasserman, "Disability, Discrimination, and Fairness," *Report from the Institute for Philosophy and Public Policy*, Winter/Spring 1993. Reprinted by permission of the institute.

It is widely agreed that people with disabilities are treated unfairly in our society: that they are the victims of pervasive discrimination, and that they have been denied adequate accommodation in areas ranging from housing construction to hiring practices to public transportation. As Congress declared in enacting the Americans with Disabilities Act (ADA) in 1990:

> [I]ndividuals with disabilities are a discrete and insular minority who have been faced with restrictions and limitations, *subjected to a history of purposeful unequal treatment*, and relegated to a position of political powerlessness in our society. . . . [emphasis added]

Yet people with disabilities were largely bypassed by the civil rights revolution of the past generation. Congress found that "unlike individuals who have experienced discrimination on the basis of race, color, sex, national origin, religion, or age, individuals who have experienced discrimination on the basis of disability have often had no legal recourse to redress such discrimination."

Reasonable Accommodation and Discrimination

The ADA is intended to provide that legal recourse. It requires employers, transit systems and public facilities to modify their operations, procedures, and physical structures so as to make reasonable accommodation for people with disabilities. The ADA recognizes broad exceptions in cases where these modifications would result in "undue hardship" or pose risks to third parties. But in principle, the statute treats the failure to ensure that people with disabilities have an "equal opportunity to benefit" from a wide range of activities and services as a form of discrimination.

The ADA's antidiscrimination framework serves several important functions. It emphasizes similarities between the treatment of people with disabilities and the treatment of other minorities. It encourages society to find the source of the disadvantages experienced by people with disabilities in its own attitudes and practices, rather than in the disabilities themselves, and it supports the proposition that accommodating people with disabilities is a matter of justice, not charity.

But the antidiscrimination model offers little guidance on how much accommodation justice requires in the face of limited resources and severe disabilities. Its requirement of equal opportunity to benefit is ambiguous, and its emphasis on remedial action by private individuals and organizations overlooks our collective responsibility for constructing a more accommodating environment. The difficult problems of social justice raised by disabilities cannot be resolved by a simple injunction against discrimination.

The ADA has obvious similarities with recent civil rights legislation. It is designed to protect members of a group long subject to exclusion and prejudice, and it does this by removing barriers to the employment and accommodation of that group. The ADA recognizes that people with disabilities have suffered from false beliefs about their capacities, just as blacks and women have, and that their exclusion has been insidiously self-perpetuating, denying them the experience needed to overcome such biases. . . .

Like earlier civil rights law, the ADA recognizes that such deeply embedded prejudice will work its way into the design of social structures and practices, and that stringent measures may be necessary to root it out. The enduring and pervasive impact of prejudice has long prompted the courts to give close scrutiny to "facially neutral" policies with an adverse impact on mistreated and disfavored groups. If public officials, for example, decide that children should attend schools in their own neighborhoods, this may appear to be a neutral basis for school assignment, but in fact it perpetuates the effects of residential covenants and other discriminatory practices that have kept minority families out of affluent suburban communities. Forced busing is not intended to achieve racially diverse schools *per se*, but to undo the enduring effects of those practices. Similarly, affirmative action is not designed to achieve demographic representativeness so much as to surmount the barriers to employment left by generations of exclusion.

The ADA's requirement of "reasonable accommodation" serves many of the same remedial functions, helping to overcome the enduring effects of conscious and unconscious discrimination. As Gregory Kavka notes, the rationales for affirmative action under earlier civil rights law are equally applicable to reasonable accommodation under the ADA: to establish the kinds of role models and "old-boy" networks that dominant groups now enjoy; to correct for the systematic errors in evaluation that result from stereotyping and overgeneralization; and to compensate for the effects of past and ongoing injustice, such as exclusion from relevant training.

The Interaction of Disabilities and Prejudice

On the other hand, the assumption that any adverse impact can be traced to prejudice, hatred, contempt, or devaluation—to what Ronald Dworkin has called "invidious discrimination"—is clearly less tenable for disability than for race or ethnicity. The ADA itself recognizes that the physical endowment of people with disabilities contributes to their disadvantage: the statute defines disability as "physical or mental impairment" that "substantially limits [the impaired person's] pursuit of major life activities." Thus, while the ADA rightly holds the attitudes and practices of the larger society responsible for much of the limitation experienced by people with disabilities, it also recognizes an objective category of biological impairment; a person whose major life activities were limited *only* by other people's attitudes or practices would be "disabled" only in a derivative sense. The disadvantages experienced by people with disabilities arise from the interaction of their physical conditions and their social environment; those disadvantages can rarely be attributed to biology *or* social practice alone.

But this understanding of disability raises a critical question about the meaning of "equal opportunity to benefit" under the ADA. In one obvious sense, we assure equal opportunity by removing *legal* barriers to entry or access. (Keep in mind that legal barriers have, in the not-too-distant past, been oppressive and pervasive: in an era when one of the great liberal Supreme Court justices could declare that "three generations of imbeciles is enough," people with disabilities were often forbidden to work, to marry, to have children, or even to be seen in public.) Yet equal opportunity conceived as freedom from legal restriction is clearly inadequate to encompass the kind of accommodations to which people with disabilities seem entitled. A more demanding notion of equal opportunity would require us to undo the effects of invidious discrimination, past and present, de jure and de facto. But even this would fail to address the severely constricted opportunities available to many people with disabilities.

A much stronger sense of equal opportunity is suggested by the ADA's mandate to eliminate "architectural barriers" and other structural impediments to access and mobility. In order to provide equal opportunity in this sense, we must remove not only barriers imposed intentionally by law and prejudice, but also barriers imposed incidentally by designs and structures that ignore the needs of people with disabilities. We must reconstruct the social world to better accommodate the range of abilities of those who inhabit it.

Structural Accommodation and Equal Opportunity

This stronger conception of equal opportunity emerges from the feminist critique of earlier civil rights laws, with their focus on invidious discrimination. Many feminists argue that the design of physical structures and social practices to accommodate one group—able-bodied males—denies equal opportunity to everyone else. The structures and practices of our society embody a dominant norm of healthy functioning, just as they embody a dominant norm of male functioning. As Susan Wendell argues:

> In North America at least, life and work have been structured as though no one of any importance in the public world . . . has to breast-feed a baby or look after a sick child. . . . Much of the world is also structured as though everyone is physically strong . . . as though everyone can walk, hear and see well.

The public world provides stairs to the able-bodied so that they can overcome the force of gravity; it is less consistent about providing ramps so that paraplegics can do the same. To build stairs for the one group without building ramps for the second denies the latter equal opportunity to benefit.

This position was anticipated a generation ago by Jacobus ten-Broek, who argued that the right of people with disabilities "to live in the world" required comprehensive changes in our physical and social order: not just in the design of buildings and public spaces, but in the duties of care owed by "abled" pedestrians, drivers, common carriers, and property owners to people with disabilities as they travel in public spaces. The refusal to make these changes denies people with disabilities their right to live in the world—the same right that was denied to blacks and women when they were excluded from public facilities.

However, providing equal opportunity for people with disabilities involves a more ambiguous and problematic commitment than the example of stairs and ramps might suggest. Ramps cost little more than stairs and are useful for people of widely varying abilities. The same is true for most of the design standards mandated by the ADA. These standards were developed more than thirty years ago, when tenBroek was writing, and their prompt implementation at that time would have probably brought about dramatic improvements in mobility and access at very slight cost.

How Much Should Society Spend?

But other opportunities to benefit do not come so cheaply. Technology sometimes offers considerable benefits, but only at enormous cost: one thinks of the devices that allow physicist Stephen Hawking to "speak." More often, perhaps, the benefits of costly technology are slight or uncertain. Does the failure to provide quadriplegics with the latest advances in robotics deny them equal opportunity? We could spend indefinitely more on robotic research and equipment, but no matter how much we spent, the opportunities of some quadriplegics would remain severely constricted.

More broadly, we cannot reasonably expect to raise all people with disabilities to a level of functioning where they can receive the same benefit from facilities and services as able-bodied people. There are many areas of employment, transit, and public accommodation where it would be impossible to achieve absolute equality in the opportunity to benefit, and where significantly reducing inequalities in the opportunity to benefit would exhaust the resources of those charged with the task of equalization.

In addressing the issue of how much a decent society should spend to improve the opportunities of people with disabilities, an equal opportunity standard is either hopelessly ambiguous or impossibly demanding. Within the ADA, moreover, there is an unresolved tension between the equal opportunity standard it affirms and the degree of inequality that will remain acceptable under its regulatory guidelines. For example, although the public transit provisions of the statute speak of equal opportunity, the accompanying regulations will leave most people with disabilities with a far greater burden of mobility than most able-bodied people. Perhaps the regulations should require more. But however much they required, they would fall short of assuring equal mobility.

The fact of biological impairment, recognized by the ADA in its definition of disability, makes the notion of "equal opportunity to benefit" problematic. This is a serious defect in a statute that treats the denial of such opportunity as a form of discrimination.

Disability and Biological Misfortune

Recognizing impairments as biological disadvantages raises the question of the extent to which a decent society must accommodate natural misfortune. Such misfortune matters greatly in determining fair treatment within the smaller unit of the family. Consider, for instance, the father's dilemma presented by Thomas Nagel:

> Suppose I have two children, one of which is quite normal and quite happy, and the other of which suffers from a painful handicap. . . . Suppose I must decide between moving to an expensive city where the second child can receive special medical treatment and schooling, but where the family's standard of living will be lower and the neighborhood will be unpleasant and dangerous for the first child—or else moving to a pleasant semi-rural suburb where the first child . . . can have a free and agreeable life. . . . [Suppose] the gain to the first child of moving to the suburb is substantially greater than the gain to the second child of moving to the city. After all, the second child will also suffer from the family's reduced standard of living and the disagreeable environment. And the educational and therapeutic benefits will not make [the second child] happy but only less miserable. For the first child, on the other hand, the choice is between a happy life and a disagreeable one.

Because the second child is worse off, his interests have a greater urgency than those of the first child. Moving to the city would be the more egalitarian decision, and, if the difference in benefit to the two children is only slight, the fairer decision. But the urgency of the second child's interests does not give them absolute priority; we would think it unfair to the first child to reduce him to the same level of misery as the second for very slight gains in the second child's well-being.

This dilemma is writ large in the allocation of educational resources for children with learning disabilities. Special education is very expensive, and many financially strapped school systems find that providing more than minimal benefit to severely disabled children would require drastic cutbacks in other programs, such as honors classes for gifted students. Yet the Education for All Handicapped Children Act of 1975 (EHA) mandates "free appropriate education" for all children, regardless of ability. This mandate has been variously interpreted to mean that children with disabilities must receive "some educational benefit," that they must receive benefit "commensurate" with that accorded to normal children, or that they must receive the "maximum possible" benefit.

The Costs of Not Having the ADA

In 1990, before the Americans with Disabilities Act (ADA) became law, people with disabilities often could not get a job, ride a city bus, or go to a restaurant or store. These barriers imposed staggering costs on the country. In signing the ADA, President George Bush estimated that each year federal, state and local governments spent almost $200 billion to support people with disabilities.

When it passed the law, Congress found that an overwhelming majority of individuals with disabilities lived in isolation and dependence. And it recognized that when store owners or employers excluded people because of their disabilities, civil rights laws were simply inadequate to redress this discrimination.

Janet Reno and Dick Thornburgh, *Wall Street Journal*, July 26, 1995.

William Galston makes a powerful argument for a commensurate benefit standard:

> In spite of profound differences among individuals, the full development of each individual—however great or limited his or her natural capacities—is equal in moral weight to that of every other. . . . [A] policy that neglects the educable retarded so that they do not learn how to care for themselves and must be institutionalized is, considered in itself, as bad as one that deprives extraordinary gifts of their chance to flower.

But technology makes "natural capacity" and "full development" very elastic notions, and this raises serious problems for a standard of equal opportunity that requires a comparison of actual and potential development.

If a society were a family, some loss of educational benefit to the most gifted students might seem justified in a school system intent upon enhancing opportunity for students with disabilities. But even in that case, an allocation that left the most gifted at the same low level of educational development as the most grievously disabled would seem grossly unfair. And it is not clear that even the modest sacrifices that would be appropriate within a family would be appropriate for the larger society; perhaps one feature that distinguishes families from larger, impersonal social units is a greater concern for the welfare of each member than for each one's share of external resources.

Who Should Bear the Costs?

Clearly, biological misfortune raises issues about the meaning of fair treatment that the ADA's antidiscrimination framework gives us little guidance in resolving. That framework also limits the social response to disabilities by imposing the costs of accommodation primarily on individuals. As we saw in the case of special education, the larger society may not always be able to bear such costs. But in other cases, burdens that would be excessive for an individual or agency may well be reasonable for a city or state. An individual should not have to plead undue hardship in order to avoid costs properly imposed on the community; a person with disabilities should not be denied accommodation because it imposes an undue hardship on an individual employer.

A 1992 analysis by Richard V. Burkhauser of the employment provisions of the ADA predicted that its antidiscrimination framework would have the effect of confining its benefits to a "disability elite"—those workers "who have the least serious disabilities and the strongest education, training, and job skills." Because employers have to bear the costs of accommodation, they will "skim the 'cream' of the population with disabilities," bypassing those with more severe and debilitating conditions. In order to help those with the most serious and pervasive disabilities, the government must significantly increase its investments in welfare, employer subsidies, and job training. But such measures are matters of distributive justice, and the fact that they are not among the remedies mandated by the ADA suggests the limitations of the antidiscrimination model upon which the current law rests.

Nevertheless, the specific provisions of the ADA on employment, transit, and public accommodation reflect, in Chief Justice Earl Warren's famous phrase, "the evolving standards of decency that mark the progress of a maturing society." To say that the question of fair treatment for people with disabilities does not have an obvious or final answer is not to say that we cannot reach a consensus on what fairness requires at our level of affluence and technological development. The ADA represents a major step towards achieving such a consensus.

Periodical Bibliography

The following articles have been selected to supplement the diverse views presented in this chapter. Addresses are provided for periodicals not indexed in the *Readers' Guide to Periodical Literature*, the *Alternative Press Index*, or the *Social Sciences Index*.

Susan Au Allen	"The New Palladium," *Vital Speeches of the Day*, September 1, 1994.
James Bovard	"The Disabilities Act's Parade of Absurdities," *Wall Street Journal*, June 22, 1995.
James I. Charlton	"The Disability Rights Movement and the Left," *Monthly Review*, July/August 1994.
Edward H. Crane	"The Social Contract Reconsidered," *Vital Speeches of the Day*, November 1, 1994.
Edwin J. Feulner	"Fear and Freedom," *Vital Speeches of the Day*, July 1, 1994.
Wray Herbert	"Our Identity Crisis," *U.S. News & World Report*, March 6, 1995.
Michael S. Joyce	"Taking Control of Our Lives Again," *USA Today*, May 1994.
Wendy Kaminer	"Feminism's Identity Crisis," *Atlantic Monthly*, October 1993.
Elizabeth Kiss	"Alchemy or Fool's Gold?" *Dissent*, Summer 1995.
John Leo	"The Spread of Rights Babble," *U.S. News & World Report*, June 28, 1993.
R. Shep Melnick	"Interpreting Entitlements: The Politics of Statutory Construction," *Brookings Review*, Winter 1994.
Fred Siegel	"Nothing in Moderation," *Atlantic Monthly*, May 1990.
Naomi Wolf	"Are Opinions Male?" *New Republic*, November 29, 1993.
Alan Wolfe	"Whose Body Politic?" *American Prospect*, Winter 1993. Available from PO Box 383080, Cambridge, MA 02238.

Does the Recovery Movement Create Victims?

Chapter Preface

A number of psychologists and authors of self-help books have popularized the concept of recovered memory: the idea that memories of traumatic events—usually chronic sexual abuse—can be repressed by victims for decades and later be vividly recalled with the help of therapy. But a growing movement—made up primarily of parents whose children have accused them of committing abuse—claims that recovered memory therapy and the self-help books that promote the concept are prompting people to falsely believe that they are victims of abuse.

Carol Tavris, social psychologist and author of *The Mismeasure of Woman*, is among many who criticize the theory of recovered memory and the self-help books aimed at survivors of child sexual abuse. While Tavris acknowledges that child abuse is a serious and underreported problem, she argues that self-help books foster the belief that *every* woman who experiences emotional difficulties must be a victim of child abuse. Moreover, she contends, many self-help books promote the potentially harmful idea that, as she puts it, "if you can't actually remember the abuse, that's all the more evidence that it happened to you." Taking issue with the concept of repressed memory, Tavris contends that writers of self-help books encourage victims to "remember" abuse that may not have occurred in order to recover from it. "The problem [with recovery manuals]," Tavris concludes, "is not with the advice they offer to victims, but with their effort to *create* victims."

Judith Lewis Herman, psychiatrist and author of *Trauma and Recovery*, praises self-help books, declaring that they "serve a valuable social purpose. They reach millions of people who feel isolated and ashamed, bringing them words of compassion and understanding." Herman and others defend the validity of the concept of repressed memory, arguing that child abuse is so horrifying that many victims develop a post-traumatic stress syndrome that causes them to temporarily lose conscious memory of the abuse. E. Sue Blume, author of the self-help book *Secret Survivors: Uncovering Incest and Its Aftereffects in Women*, disputes the charge that self-help books "create" victims: "There is no evidence that anyone who was not sexually abused can be persuaded otherwise, let alone made to suffer post-incest syndrome." Blume, Herman, and others in the self-help movement argue that when victims recognize that they have repressed memories, they are able to stop denying that they were abused and to begin the process of recovering from the abuse.

The viewpoints in the following chapter present differing views on whether the recovery movement creates victims or helps them to overcome abuse and addictions.

> "Codependency offers a diagnosis, and support group, to virtually anyone with a problem who can read."

The Recovery Movement Undermines Personal Responsibility in Addicts

Wendy Kaminer

The growth of recovery and self-actualization movements, modeled on the twelve-step program of Alcoholics Anonymous, has fueled a boom in the publication of self-help books. In the following viewpoint, Wendy Kaminer argues that authors of self-help books, by stretching the concept of codependency to cover everyone, offer simplistic advice that undermines in addicts the personal responsibility that is necessary for recovery. Kaminer is the author of books on feminism and criminal justice, as well as *I'm Dysfunctional, You're Dysfunctional: The Recovery Movement and Other Self-Help Fashions*.

As you read, consider the following questions:

1. How do authors Melody Beattie and Anne Wilson Schaef define codependency, according to Kaminer?
2. According to the author, why is personal experience with addiction as important as a professional degree to self-help writers?
3. How does Kaminer define the inner child?

Excerpted from "Chances Are You're Codependent Too" by Wendy Kaminer, *New York Times Book Review*, February 11, 1990. An expanded version of this article appears in the author's book *I'm Dysfunctional, You're Dysfunctional: The Recovery Movement and Other Self-Help Fashions* (Reading, MA: Addison-Wesley, 1992).

Instead of a self-help section, my local bookstore has a section called Recovery, right around the corner from the one called New Age. It's stocked with books about addiction, psychic healing and codependency—a popular new disease blamed for such diverse disorders as drug abuse, alcoholism, anorexia, child abuse, compulsive gambling, chronic lateness, fear of intimacy and low self-esteem. Codependency, which originally referred to the problems of people married to alcoholics, was discovered by self-actualization experts around 1985, and redefined. Now it applies to any problem associated with any addiction suffered by you or someone close to you. This amorphous disease is a business, generating millions of book sales, countless support groups and, in September 1989, the First National Conference on Codependency in Scottsdale, Arizona. Codependency "has arrived," according to a conference report; recovery is a national grassroots movement.

Defining Codependency

Codependency is advertised as a national epidemic, partly because every conceivable form of arguably compulsive behavior is classified as an addiction. (We are a nation of sexaholics, rageaholics, shopaholics, and rushaholics.) "I have a feeling we're soon going to have special groups for third cousins of excessive sherry drinkers," the child psychologist Robert Coles told me. "You don't know whether to laugh or cry about this stuff." The codependency movement has "run amok," he said. It's a "typical example of how anything packaged as psychology in this culture seems to have an all too gullible audience."

The codependency movement also exemplifies our fears of an enemy within and the demonization of addiction and disease. What were once billed as bad habits and problems—Cinderella and Peter Pan complexes, smart women loving too much and making foolish choices about men who hate them—are now considered addictions too, or reactions to the addictions of others, or both. Like drug and alcohol abuse, they're considered codependent diseases. If the self-help industry is any measure of our state of mind in 1990, we are indeed obsessed with disease and our will to defeat it: all codependency books stress the curative power of faith and self-discipline. It's morning after in America; we want to be in recovery.

Almost everyone—96 percent of Americans—suffers from codependency, these self-proclaimed experts assert, and given their very broad definitions of this disease, we probably do. Melody Beattie, the best-selling author of *Codependent No More* and *Beyond Codependency*, defines codependency as being affected by someone else's behavior and obsessed with controlling it. Who isn't? Another definition comes from Anne Wilson Shaef, the

95

author of the best-selling *When Society Becomes an Addict* and *Co-dependence: Misunderstood—Mistreated,* who calls it "a disease process whose assumptions, beliefs and lack of spiritual awareness lead to a process of nonliving which is progressive."

That some readers think they know what this means is a tribute to what George Orwell considered reduced expectations of language and the substitution of attitudes and feeling for ideas. It is enough for Ms. Schaef to mean that codependency is bad and anyone can have it, which makes this condition seem more like a marketing device. Codependency offers a diagnosis, and support group, to virtually anyone with a problem who can read. . . .

Codependency and the Family

What's striking about all the codependency books on the market (I've read twenty-one) is their sameness. They may differ in levels of literacy and how they balance the discussion of codependency theory with recovery techniques. But they describe the same syndromes in the same jargon and prescribe the same cure—enlistment in a support group that follows an overtly religious recovery program (stressing submission to a higher power) borrowed from Alcoholics Anonymous (A.A.). Codependency books line the shelves in bookstores like different brands of aspirin in a drugstore. As Peter Vegso, president of Health Communications, Inc., said, "A lot of people are looking at why they're not happy."

Their unhappiness begins at home, in the dysfunctional family, codependency authors stress, drawing heavily on family systems theory, explaining the way individuals develop in relation or reaction to their families. Codependency is attributed to child abuse, which makes it an intergenerational familial disease; child abuse defined broadly to include any emotional or physical abandonment, disrespect or inadequate nurturance, begets child abuse, or anorexia and other forms of self-abuse. This is surely part of codependency's appeal. We are all fascinated by our families. No soap opera is more compelling than our own.

Codependency books lead readers back through childhood to discover the ways in which they've been abused and the "negative messages" they've internalized. Exercises, quizzes and sentence-completion tests (for example," I have trouble owning my feeling reality around my father when . . .") assist readers in self-evaluation. You can estimate you codependency score, your place on a "worry index" or your PTSD (post-traumatic stress disorder) average. You can find your own pattern or syndrome in the usual assortment of case studies that track the children of abuse into adulthood. Readers are encouraged to reconstruct their pasts by drawing family trees that chart their legacy of disease; grandfather is an alcoholic, mother is a compulsive rescuer and Uncle Murray weighs 270 pounds; father is a sex addict, your sister is anorexic and you only have affairs with married men.

Still, encased in silliness and jargon are some sound, potentially helpful insights into how character takes shape in the drama of family life. Codependency literature may reflect some of the often criticized selfism of the 1970s. (Ms. Beattie dedicates *Codependent No More* "to me.") But accusing self-help authors of selfism is like accusing fiction writers of making things up, and the concept of codependency does combine concern for self with the more recent focus on family and community. The self is never viewed in isolation; codependency theory places the struggle for individual identity in the context of familial relations.

"We cannot have an identity all alone," John Bradshaw writes in *Bradshaw On: The Family*. "Our reality is shaped from the beginning by a *relationship*." Children in dysfunctional families are shaped by bad relationships and are improperly "individuated." (Codependents are always said to suffer from "boundary" problems, confusion about where they end and other people begin.) Dysfunctional families sacrifice their members to the family system, Mr. Bradshaw suggests, in one of the more cogent explanations of codependency: *"The individual exists to keep the system in balance."* . . .

Codependency and Society

Society itself is addicted to (among the other things mentioned in these books) the arms race, the repression of emotion, the accumulation of capital and enlarging the hole in the ozone layer. These "addictions" partly reflect what is implicitly condemned as the disease of masculinity: rationalist left-brain thinking. As Ms. Shaef explains in *When Society Becomes an Addict*, the "White Male System" is addictive, and it's the only system we know.

This view of codependency as a pervasive, institutionalized disease not only provides codependency authors with the widest possible audience—everyone—it imbues them with messianic zeal. Codependency is, after all, considered fatal, for individuals, corporations and the nation. It causes cancer and other stress-related diseases, these books warn, as well as business failures, environmental pollution and war.

If society and everyone in it are addicted, self-destructing, infected with left-brain rationality, then people in recovery are the chosen few, an elite minority of enlightened, if irrational, self-actualizers with the wisdom to save the world. As Ms. Schaef confirms, the only people who can help cure our addictive system are those "recovering from the effects."

Experts themselves must thus admit that they're recovering codependents too, and codependency books tend to be partly confessional, following a model of the expert as patient taken from A.A.: "Hello! My name is Carla and I am recovering from just about every addiction known to humanity," Carla Wills-Brandon perkily reveals at the beginning of *Is It Love or Is It Sex?* Personal experience with addiction and recovery is as important a credential as professional degrees, partly because the therapeutic profession itself is considered a nest of practicing codependents. Lynne Namka, the author of *The Doormat Syndrome*, advises you to choose a therapist "who has fewer psychological problems than you do."

Self-Help Books Offer Simplistic Advice

As individual works of confession and advice, abuse-survivor books are often reassuring and supportive. They encourage victims of childhood molestation to speak up, to understand that they are not alone and to find help. The problem is not with the advice they offer to victims, but with their effort to *create* victims—to expand the market that can then be treated with therapy and self-help books. To do this, survival books all hew to a formula based on an uncritical acceptance of certain premises about the nature of memory and trauma. They offer simple answers at a time when research psychologists are posing hard questions.

Carol Tavris, the *New York Times Book Review*, January 3, 1993.

But if they decline to cloak themselves in the power of professional expertise, these writers who've "been there" invoke the moral authority we grant survivors. Everyone wants to be a survivor, as if survivalhood were the only alternative to victimization. "QUAKE SURVIVOR RELOCATES seeks 'humanistic' male," a personal ad in the the *New York Review of Books* explains. "I survived" the subway strike, the summer of '88, Hurricane Hugo, T-shirts attest. "I survived codependency," people in recovery may boast like figures at a *New Yorker* cartoon cocktail party. In recovery there are no victims—of incest, drug abuse, or love—there are only survivors.

Recovery and the Inner Child

The process of recovery (it's not an event, these experts repeatedly explain) brings even more than survival. The recovery "lifestyle" eventually brings rebirth. Its goal is healing your inner child—the wounded child who took refuge from abuse and deprivation in a recess of your soul.

Or, perhaps the inner child *is* the soul. *"We all carry within us an eternal child,"* Jeremiah Abrams writes in his introduction to

Reclaiming the Inner Child, an eclectic anthology of academic and pop essays about the child within that are alternately eloquent, intelligent, trite and incomprehensible. Inner-child theory is an equally eclectic synthesis of Carl Jung, New Age mysticism, holy-children mythology, pop psychology and psychoanalytic theories about narcissism and the creation of a false self that wears emotions without experiencing them.

Codependency, which includes narcissism, is generally described as a failure to feel, or a failure to feel what's true. Addiction masks true feeling and the true, childlike self. Codependents are considered adult children. If some behave more like Scrooge than Peter Pan, all have a Tiny Tim within.

Inner children are always good—innocent and pure—like the most sentimentalized Dickens characters, which means that most people are essentially good and, most of all, redeemable. Even Ayatollah Khomeini [of Iran] had a child within. Think of little Adolf Hitler abandoned in his crib. Evil is merely a mask of dysfunction.

The therapeutic view of evil as sickness, not sin, is particularly strong in codependency theory. Shaming children, calling them bad, is a primary form of abuse. Both guilt and shame "are not useful as a way of life," Ms. Beattie writes in *Codependent No More*. "We need to forgive ourselves. . . . Guilt makes *everything* harder." This is not moral relativism; distinctions are made between healthy and unhealthy behavior. It reflects instead the need to believe that no one is unforgivable and everyone can be saved. Because within every addict there's a holy child yearning to be free, recovery holds the promise of redemption. . . .

Recovery and Conformity

In the self-help universe, anyone can be healthy, spiritually centered, rich and thin—with faith, self-discipline and the willingness to take direction. This hopeful pragmatism is supposed to be singularly American, and we tend to be as proud of the self-help tradition as we are enamored of the notion that we are a country of people forever inventing ourselves.

But if the how-to phenomenon reflects a democratic belief in the power of will to overcome circumstances of nature and class, it's built on an authoritarian mystique of expertise that encourages conformity. Experts pretend to divulge secrets to readers, mystifying the obvious jargon and italics. Experts are always unique (their tritest pronouncements are packaged as news), but readers are fungible, suffering the same syndromes and needful of the same cures. Self-help book collectivize the process of identity formation, exploiting readers' fears of embarking on the search for self without the aid of exercise techniques, assurances of success and, of course, support groups.

To criticize the conformity implicit in self-help, you needn't deny the solace people find in collectivity or suggest that they are better off pursuing their addictions individually than curing them in groups. You needn't question the sincerity of recovery proselytizers or even the benefits offered by a few profiteers: we are all better off if addicts consume only books. We will all survive recovery. But what of the passivity and search for simple absolutes the recovery movement reflects?

Codependency authors say that recovery is ultimately an individual journey, but readers are not expected to find their paths or their transport techniques alone. There is little solitude and no isolation in recovery: outside your support group you're with God. Recovery requires much less than self-help; it requires self-surrender, to a higher power or cosmic truth or other non-denominational universal force.

This isn't the narcissism commonly associated with self-help so much as submission; it isn't individualism so much as a hunger to belong. The putative message of codependency—that we are responsible for ourselves and shouldn't spend our lives heeding or pleasing others—is undermined by the medium in which it's conveyed. Merely buying a self-help book is an act of dependence, a refusal to confront the complexities of a solitary creative effort, as well as its failures.

"Many people learn to face life on life's terms only after they have ended the reliance on an overly dependent or destructively dependent relationship."

The Recovery Movement Helps People Overcome Addiction

Steve Hamilton

The reputed success of Alcoholics Anonymous in the treatment of alcoholism generated a proliferation of similar programs for those recovering from other addictions and spawned a recovery movement. In the following viewpoint, Steve Hamilton contends that this recovery movement, with its concepts of codependence and "adult children," helps people to overcome not only addictions but also the detrimental effects of abusive relationships. Hamilton is a licensed marriage, family, and child counselor in San Francisco, California.

As you read, consider the following questions:

1. In the author's opinion, why does the Alcoholics Anonymous approach work so well with alcoholics and addicts?
2. What is the modern definition of addiction adopted by the recovery movement, according to Hamilton?
3. How has the concept of codependence been broadened, according to the author?

Excerpted from Steve Hamilton, "Getting with the Program," *Crossroads*, April 1993. Reprinted by permission of *Crossroads*.

Since its inception in the 1930s, Alcoholics Anonymous (AA) has quietly grown as a "spiritual program" of alcohol recovery. For years, most people knew little about AA or "12-Step" programs but respected a program that seemed to work. Even psychotherapists, initially wary of infringement on their territory, grew increasingly willing to steer substance abusers in this direction because they recognized that AA's unique combination of peer support and philosophical structure was more effective for many alcoholics than traditional psychotherapy. Whatever one thought personally of AA's religious-philosophical framework didn't seem to matter.

During the last decade, Alcoholics Anonymous and other 12-Step programs have grown enormously. Previously targeted at a particular subpopulation, they are now at the heart of a "Recovery Movement" that has dominated U.S. popular psychology since the mid-1980s. The accompanying development of Adult Children of Alcoholics (ACA) and the enormous popularity of this and similar programs (note the extent to which terms like "co-alcoholic" have entered the popular vocabulary) have forged something approximating a generalized theory of human personality and social relationships.

This movement has translated into a "recovery movement" in its own right for the U.S. health care system, providing the only profitable units in some hospital systems. The competitive field of psychotherapy has gotten into the act as well, as shown by the proliferation of slick brochures promising to unfold the secret to "finding the hidden child within" and why you "love too much." But what is the significance of this ideology on popular—and political—culture?

Alcoholics Anonymous

AA was largely the originator of the peer-support-group model for treatment of addiction. The other members of the group have experienced the same problems the individual is facing, so they can model ways to effectively deal with them, and their support can have a powerful emotional impact. This factor alone can provide the spark for the individual to quickly take responsibility for his or her recovery.

The support group thus provides a therapeutic community in which advice and support is available. Group values and expectations define maintenance of sobriety as the most important goal for the individual and the criterion, in effect, for inclusion in the group. (Sometimes this focus is a bit myopic, negating almost entirely the value of the individual's life prior to recovery and defining the addiction to alcohol as the root of all his or her problems, even in years of sobriety.) But for those who have the "openness" and "willingness" to "apply themselves to this simple

102

program," the new value system takes hold. An individual who may have been isolated or who had an unreliable network of friends becomes engaged in a new social network that shares values that encourage sobriety.

Are there reasons why this approach, which relies heavily on group culture, works so well with alcoholics and other addicts? If there is any character trait consistently associated with addicts, it is emotional dependency. Social acceptance within the AA subculture thus speaks to that dependency and channels it in a presumably positive direction. It is certainly a culture in which conformity to group values is emphasized over individual expression, although a "live and let live" attitude of tolerance often leaves room for individual eccentricity.

But in addition to finding peer support and adopting a new value system supporting sobriety, most individuals who become deeply involved in "The Program" take the 12-Step philosophy seriously and undergo something of a religious conversion. On one level, the emotional dependency, initially focused on key individuals such as sponsors and friends, becomes internalized and abstracted into a concept, the "Higher Power."

Perhaps especially for those of us who are atheists or agnostics, it is important to understand the semi-religious appeal of 12-Step programs. Unless we do so, we cannot understand why the appeal of these programs is so powerful and enduring. I think that an emotionally supportive, positive worldview and belief system is a powerful motivator, and perhaps for many a necessary prerequisite for making difficult changes in lifestyle and behavior. This is an aspect usually overlooked by traditional psychotherapy. . . .

The Addiction Model

The view of alcoholism incorporated into the AA perspective is known as the "disease model." This view, more experientially than scientifically derived, maintains that alcoholism is a progressive disease with physical, emotional and spiritual components. The spiritual and emotional components are primarily addressed in terms of the identification and removal of "character defects." Emotional and what some would call "spiritual" resources are needed to overcome the addiction. . . .

The disease model has gone through a subtle change within AA itself in recent years. Younger people have frequently turned up in AA with a history of combined drug and alcohol use, a combination that has brought them to the point of crisis much sooner than the natural course of alcohol abuse alone. Even this change in application of the paradigm necessitated some change in AA's definition, which emphasizes physiological dependence on alcohol. By the time the addiction model was stretched further to apply to dependence on such things as sex and relationships, we were really talking about a different addiction model—ironically, a much more psychological model. The modern addiction model, an interpretation of the AA model by the broader Recovery Movement, defines addiction as dependence on anything (food, sex, drugs, gambling, work) as a way of coping with life's stresses and as a way of compensating for lack of self-esteem, a repetitious and destructive pattern that is a futile attempt to make oneself feel better.

12-Step Programs Are Effective

What has made Alcoholics Anonymous's (A.A.) spirituality so effective in the lives of many people is, I believe, the specific nature of its suggestions. They embody ancient spiritual insights of many religions of both East and West and deliver them to people of the 20th century whose lives are unmanageable and who feel powerless to change them by their own devices. Such persons are trapped in various types of addictive behaviors. A.A.'s 12 steps have proved effective for compulsions other than drinking—gambling, narcotics, sex, eating and smoking, to name but a few.

Neil J. Carr, *America*, June 17, 1995.

Such a definition broadens the purview of "addiction studies" considerably. The repetitious acting out of unproductive behavior patterns is a central concern of most theories of personality, from Freud to the present. The "addiction" framework seems, at first glance, a bit simplistic but—and herein lies the popularity of this approach—it is a graspable, accessible framework for approaching an array of personal and interpersonal problems.

Addiction to Sex and Relationships

It is in the realm of sex and relationships that the addiction model has been transformed most clearly into a psychological model. Here there is no question of physiological dependency, whether inherited or acquired. One's definition of "sobriety" must also be more flexible as well, since total abstinence is not, for most people, an acceptable outcome. The core belief is that people engage in compulsive sexual activity or become involved in destructive or obsessively consuming relationships (quite different but sometimes overlapping issues) as an ultimately futile way of compensating for low self-esteem. The pattern may vary considerably, from the typical "addict" who bounces quickly from affair to affair or sexual encounter to sexual encounter to the "sexual anorexic" who longs for but fears sexual involvements, presumably to avoid giving way to an all-consuming passion.

The standard advice is borrowed from the AA model to the extent possible through a period of sexual abstinence, during which one can get one's bearings, laying the groundwork for choosing one's involvements in a more thoughtful and responsible and productive way in the future, one that is less driven and "out of control."

People often do find this framework helpful, giving them a respite from behavior that has become habitual and often harmful, and helping them to begin approaching issues of sex and relationships in a more thoughtful, conscious manner. Other aspects of 12-Step programs apply here as well, including a supportive and nonjudgmental atmosphere for honest acknowledgement of problems, peer support and examples of behavior changes.

But there are problems with the extension of the AA program. The further one gets from substance abuse and into more complicated territory such as the tendency to repeat destructive relationships, the more the "one size fits all" approach is likely to be inadequate. On this issue, most of us still have such a wellspring of sexual guilt, even though it may lie behind a facade of sexual permissiveness, that a response based to a large extent on avoidance of sex and relationships may not always be healthy. This may be especially true if our own ambivalent and complicated attempts to form relationships are judged "unhealthy" by some idealized (monogamous) standard.

Co-Dependence

The most widely applied concept regarding relationships that has spun off from the AA framework is not based on the addict, but on the one who is affected by the addict's behavior, the "co-dependent." The concept of co-dependency had its origins in Alanon, the AA-related support group for partners of alcoholics, and the term began to be used more broadly in the family therapy components of treatment programs to include those family members affected by the addiction. The earlier Alanon term "co-alcoholic" described a certain dynamic in which the nonalcoholic partner would stay in a destructive relationship, excusing and covering for the alcoholic partner, sacrificing his or her own needs in the process but often getting some secondary satisfaction from this relationship. The secondary satisfaction might be a sense of power derived from being the more functional partner or perhaps a masochistic sense of identity from being the caretaker, filling a need to be needed.

By the time this concept became popularized there was already a great danger of overgeneralization and oversimplification. People stay in such relationships for all sorts of reasons—

and not the least of which, for the women who often fit into this role, has been the lack of economic opportunities. However, there are certainly women and men who are drawn towards such caretaking relationships—and in fact, many who have never had an alcoholic partner identify with these dynamics and find support groups to address these issues.

While it can be limiting to organize one's identity totally around being an addict, it must be more limiting to define oneself in relation to the addicted partner. Not surprisingly, the concept of "co-dependency" has been broadened considerably to describe a more general orientation to relationships. Sometimes the term now simply describes a tendency to be too dependent on one's partner or on the idea of having a relationship. It is used to describe the kind of caretaking and controlling behaviors described above, or even more broadly allowing one's feelings to be affected by others' behavior and/or needing to influence others' behavior. However, the Recovery Movement needed another element to give flesh and blood and history to an approach to dealing with interpersonal problems that focused on co-dependency. Where are these behaviors learned? The origin of dysfunctional behavior was found in dysfunctional families.

Adult Children of Alcoholics

Although the 12-Step programs have expanded considerably in recent years, it has been the overnight success of Adult Children of Alcoholics (ACA) and related programs that have given the Recovery Movement its finished (and sellable) form. ACA is basically an application of family therapy principles to the alcoholic family. There are unfortunately enough alcoholic families that such an emphasis touched an easily identifiable nerve in many people. In fact, the characterizations of the dysfunctional family popularized by this approach touched a nerve in practically everyone, whether they had an alcoholic parent or not.

The child in such a family would find himself/herself enmeshed in a set of behaviors that were necessary for survival. Arbitrary, irrational, confusing and inconsistent parental behavior elicited predictable responses—sitting on one's feelings, "people pleasing," and having confused boundaries as to one's own needs and feelings and those of others. A well-defined model was established for reinterpreting early childhood experience, and it indeed led to a Pandora's box of repressed resentments and, perhaps, explanations for why adult relationships were filled with fears, ambivalence and self-defeating patterns. Part of ACA's appeal for those both inside and outside 12-Step programs was that it did provide a legitimate sense of victimization, pushing the responsibility a bit off the individual and back onto at least the family environment. For those already in 12-

Step programs, this was probably a needed space, a structured context for the exploration of feelings.

Like the family therapy approach generally, the ACA model focuses more on the typical dynamics of certain types of families than on in-depth individual or family analysis. Such an approach often has great effectiveness in quickly pinpointing, labelling and challenging many destructive patterns. The downside again lies in the lack of differentiation, the too easy "one size fits all" quality to much of the analysis and prescription for change that comes from this perspective. When people come from these meetings talking about being "co-dependent," "people pleasing" victims of a "dysfunctional" family working to "discover the hidden child within," it is tempting to think that the program is given to easy generalization. For example, a child who has been left with a neurotic sense of "badness" because for no apparent reason he elicits his father's rage may exhibit a poor sense of his own needs and rights and engage in "people pleasing" behavior in various forms. Another child, with much less in the way of bonds of love and trust established, may exhibit "people pleasing" behavior as a strategy to get his way or protect himself but be quite capable of asserting himself in other situations. Both have issues of "self-esteem," although their source and expression is not the same. To give both the advice that they should stop being "people pleasers" and go about more forcefully seeking the satisfaction of their needs will not necessarily be sufficient. The one model that tends to fit all situations involves the rejection of "people pleasing," "co-dependent" notions that any person's satisfaction may lie to any great extent on a relationship with another.

The Strength of the Co-Dependency Theory

Certainly partners and family members of alcoholics and other addicts have learned through painful experience the need to pull back and stop trying to make someone else's life work for them. They, and people in many other situations, need to learn they do not have to be abused. They often learn that the only consistent and loving choice is at some point to allow the abusive or self-destructive friend or partner to experience the consequences of his/her own behavior. Many people learn to face life on life's terms only after they have ended the reliance on an overly dependent or destructively dependent relationship. Only then do they identify and learn to express their own feelings and needs. They learn to stop living life to meet other's expectations, to establish their own expectations and goals. This is the strength of the current emphasis on "co-dependency." . . .

Some have seen in Alcoholics Anonymous and its offshoots a complete "psychologizing" of America—that is, the triumph, on a popular level, of introspective analysis and emotional adaptation ("accept life on life's own terms") over critical social analysis and activism. If this is true, however, it is not the bored introspection of the middle class, but, in many cases, a manifestation of struggle for physical and emotional survival from the ravages of alcoholism, drug addiction, and psychological infirmities that are so endemic to this society.

"*[The recovery movement's] main intended audience is women who aren't at all sure that they were molested, and its purpose is to convince them of that fact.*"

Repressed Memory Therapy Creates Victims

Frederick Crews

Some psychotherapists and popular authors contend that memories of traumatic events—such as chronic sexual abuse—can be repressed for decades and later be vividly recalled by victims in therapy. In the following viewpoint, Frederick Crews argues that the theory of repressed memories has no scientific basis; rather, he asserts, "false memories" are planted in patients by overzealous therapists. Repressed memory therapy, according to Crews, has a detrimental effect on the women who are tricked into believing these false memories. Crews is a professor of English and chair of the English department at the University of California, Berkeley.

As you read, consider the following questions:

1. According to Crews, what percentage of American women do leaders of the recovery movement claim are victims of abuse?
2. How does the author define abreaction?
3. According to Ofshe and Watters, cited by the author, what is the real tragedy of false memories?

From *The Revenge of the Repressed: Part 2.* Copyright ©1994 by Frederick Crews. Originally appeared in the *New York Review of Books*, December 1, 1994. Reprinted by permission of Lescher & Lescher, Ltd., for the author.

Throughout the American 1980s and beyond, the interrogation of small children for their memories of recent sexual abuse played a role in many a criminal case against accused molesters who had not, in fact, done anything wrong. The social and financial costs have been enormous. To take only the most famous example, staff members of the McMartin Preschool in Manhattan Beach, California, who were accused of every imaginable horror associated with devil worship, had to endure the longest (almost seven years [1983 to 1990]) and most expensive ($15 million) trial in American history before the case collapsed from the weight of its accumulated absurdities. In other instances, draconian sentences are being served and plea bargains are still being coerced in the face of transparently clear signs that the charges are bogus. Even today, our criminal justice system is just beginning to erect safeguards against the error that makes such outrages possible: the assumption that children are still reliable witnesses after exposure to their parents' and inquisitors' not-so-subtle hints that certain kinds of revelations are expected of them.

Not even that much progress, however, is being made with respect to curbing parallel travesties involving the therapeutically manufactured memories of adults who decide that they must have been molested in their own childhood. On the contrary: by extending their statutes of limitations to allow for thirty years and more of non-recollection, our states have been codifying a pseudoscientific notion of repressed-yet-vividly-retrieved memory that can cause not merely injustice but enormous grief and havoc. Obviously, the impetus for such legislative backwardness is not coming from reputable psychological research—which offers no support to the concept of repression even in its mildest form. The momentum comes rather from a combination of broad popular belief and a relatively narrow but intense crusading fervor.

The Beginning of a Movement

Since 1988, the most successful communicators of both the belief and the fervor have been Ellen Bass and Laura Davis, coauthors of the "recovery manual" *The Courage to Heal*. A teacher of creative writing and her student, Bass and Davis were radical feminists who lacked any background in psychology. Their knowledge base consisted of stories they had heard from women who clearly remembered that they had been sexually abused in childhood but who had been rebuffed by uncaring therapists and family members. Noting the high numbers of such cases reported within women's collectives, and further noting that other women in such groups eventually produced incest "memories" of their own, Bass and Davis soon decided that repressed abuse must be even more pervasive than remembered abuse. The more likely explanation of the late-blooming cases—namely, that the dynamics of the group encouraged false memory formation by making victimhood into a test of authentic belonging—has yet to dawn on these collaborators.

Precisely because their minds were unclouded by research findings, Bass and Davis uncannily reflected the ideological spirit of their moment and milieu. As Mark Pendergrast relates in *Victims of Memory*, the mounting (and very legitimate) concern about the underreported incidence of real child molestation formed only one corner of the picture. Bass and Davis also spoke to a public mood of impatient moral absolutism; an obsession with the themes, popularized by John Bradshaw [author of *Bradshaw On: The Family*] and others, of codependency, the "dysfunctional family," and the "inner child"; a widespread susceptibility to occult beliefs; the rise of "lookism" and other manifestations of hypersensitivity to the violation of personal space; and the angry conviction in some quarters that all men are rapists at heart. While Andrea Dworkin [author of *Pornography: Men Possessing Women*] and Susan Brownmiller [author of *Against Our Will: Men, Women and Rape*] were hypothesizing that American fathers regularly rape their daughters in order to teach them what it means to be inferior, Bass and Davis set about to succor the tens of millions of victims who must have repressed that ordeal.

Recovered Memory Therapy Creates Monsters

Recently, a new miracle "cure" has been promoted by some mental health professionals—recovered memory therapy. This treatment leads clients to see their parents as monsters who sexually abused them as children. Parents have to witness their adult children turn into monsters trying to destroy their reputations and lives. In less than ten years' time this therapy, in its various forms, has devastated thousands of lives. It has become a nationwide phenomenon—one that is becoming entrenched in our culture and the mental health professions with enormous speed.

Richard Ofshe and Ethan Watters, *Society*, March/April 1993.

No single book, of course, can make a social movement. Although *The Courage to Heal* had already sold over three quarters of a million copies before its third edition appeared in 1994, and although its spinoff volumes constitute a small industry in their own right, Bass and Davis have been joined by a considerable number of other writers who share their slant. (Other key movement documents include Renee Fredrickson, *Repressed Memo-*

ries: *A Journey to Recovery from Sexual Abuse*; E. Sue Blume, *Secret Survivors: Uncovering Incest and Its Aftereffects in Women*; and Patricia Love, *The Emotional Incest Syndrome: What To Do When a Parent's Love Rules Your Life*.) Moreover, the recovered memory business quickly outgrew the motives of its founders. By now it has evolved into a highly lucrative enterprise not just of therapy and publishing but also of counseling, workshop hosting, custody litigation, criminal prosecution, forced hospitalization, and insurance and "victim compensation" claims.

The Extent of Sexual Abuse

The recovery movement, it must be plainly understood, is not primarily addressed to people who always knew about their sexual victimization. Its main intended audience is women who aren't at all sure that they were molested, and its purpose is to convince them of that fact and embolden them to act upon it. As for genuine victims, the comfort they are proffered may look attractive at first, but it is of debatable long-term value. *The Courage to Heal* and its fellow manuals are not about surmounting one's tragic girlhood but about keeping the psychic wounds open, refusing forgiveness or reconciliation, and joining the permanently embittered corps of "survivors."

In the eyes of the recovery movement's leaders, as many as half of all American women are veterans of sexual abuse. If so, the logic seems to run, you can hardly fail to unearth a victim wherever you look and by however desultory a means of detection. But a revealing game with definitions is being played here. For writers like Bass and Davis, Renee Fredrickson, and E. Sue Blume, sexual molestation occurs whenever the victim thinks— or later comes to believe that she must have thought—that an inappropriate kind of contact is occurring. Blume, indeed, denies that physical touching need be involved at all. "Incest," she explains, "can occur through words, sounds, or even exposure of the child to sights or acts that are sexual but do not involve her." And still another movement writer, Love, denounces what she calls "emotional incest," which can be committed by parents who "appear loving and devoted," "spend a great deal of time with their children and lavish them with praise and material gifts," but do so merely "as an unconscious ploy to satisfy their own unmet needs."

False Positives and the "Backlash"

From the standpoint of public health, what's most disturbing here is a likely growth in the number of "false positives"—women who were never molested but who are enticed into believing that they were. The mavens of recovered memory concern themselves almost entirely with means of *reinforcing* incest suspicions, not with means of checking them against solid evidence pro or con. Their advice to friends and counselors of a woman who has been led to suspect early molestation is generally the same: never cast doubt on those suspicions. So, too, she herself is urged to stifle all doubts. In Renee Fredrickson's words, "You may be convinced that your disbelief is a rational questioning of the reality versus unreality of your memories, but it is partially a misguided attempt to repress the memories again."

It is little wonder, then, that Bass and Davis, through the first two editions of *The Courage to Heal,* had yet to encounter a single woman who "suspected she might have been abused, explored it, and determined that she wasn't." Now, in a third edition that is beginning to sound nervous about "the backlash" in general and pending damage suits in particular, it is admitted that some therapists "have pushed clients to acknowledge abuse . . . that did not occur." But even those few bad apples, in Bass and Davis's still erroneous judgment, cannot "create new memories in their clients"; and the women who change their minds after leaving therapy "represent only a tiny fraction of the millions of actual survivors. . . ."

The "false positives" problem has been exacerbated by the checklists of telltale symptoms that adorn the movement's self-help manuals and advice columns. Smarting from criticism of their earlier checklists, Bass and Davis adopt a warier posture now; nevertheless, they still leave the implication that if you "feel different from other people," incest is a likely cause. E. Sue Blume tells you that you were probably molested if you speak too softly, or wear too many clothes, or have "no awareness at all" of having been violated. If you have checked the questionnaire items "I neglect my teeth" or "There are certain things I seem to have a strange affection or attraction for," Renee Fredrickson knows why. And according to the ubiquitous John Bradshaw, a victim can be spotted either by her sexual promiscuity or, as the case may be, by her lack of interest in sex. These are all sterling examples of what experimentally minded psychologists dryly call a "confirmatory bias.". . .

Therapy's Detrimental Effects

The recovery movement's feminist affinity should not lead anyone to suppose that its incitement to militant victimhood serves the best interests of women. It is precisely women who make up most of the movement's casualties. Once a patient is invited to believe that her inner child was suffocated at an early age, she may well put the major blame on her mother; that is just what we see in a significant minority of cases. Estrangement between sisters—one converted to hellishly revised memories of their years together, the other refusing to go along—is also a regular aftermath of therapy. But above all, the chief sufferer usually turns out to be the female patient herself.

Recovery manuals preach the doctrine of "abreaction," whereby a patient must painfully relive each repressed memory if she is to stand a chance of freeing herself from it. The experience is guaranteed to be rough. In Lenore Terr's version of this truth [*Unchained Memories: True Stories of Traumatic Memories, Lost and Found*], "Clinicians find that once repression lifts, individuals become far more symptomatic. They become anxious, depressed, sometimes suicidal, and far more fearful of items suggestive of their traumas." Bass and Davis agree. "Don't hurt or try to kill yourself . . . ," they feel compelled to advise. "Sit tight and ride out the storm." For many women, however, the storm doesn't end, or else it ends all too abruptly with suicide. And even in the best of cases, a "survivor" is coached to reject the happiest actual memories of her childhood as being inconsistent with the stark truth of molestation. The result is a lasting sacrifice of resilience, security of identity, humor, capacity to show affection, and connection to the people who have cared most steadily about this woman's happiness. . . .

Psychotherapy Creates Victims

Making Monsters: False Memories, Psychotherapy, and Sexual Hysteria, by Richard Ofshe and Ethan Watters, is finely attuned to the thralldom that would-be healers impose upon their clients, whose mundane initial complaints are typically supplanted by anxiety, suggestibility, and a desperate dependency. What distinguishes this book is its focus on the resultant psychological transformation of patients. For Ofshe and Watters, the speciousness of the so-called memories is incidental to the real tragedy, a "brutalization and psychological torture" of people who get stripped of their actual early memories, infused with fanatical hatred of their parents, and disabled for normal coping in the world beyond the drifting lifeboat of survivorship. The patients themselves become grotesque in the very act of "making monsters" out of the people who nurtured them.

Ofshe and Watters offer us the clearest account of how the very inefficacy of memory treatment—its indefinite postponing of an expected self-restoration—can lock the patient and therapist in an ever more macabre embrace. Thus:

> Therapists often find themselves forced to explain why, after the first series of recovered memories, the client's symptoms do not disappear as promised. The easiest answer is to presume that the abuse must have been more serious than originally thought, and that more repressed memories are hidden in the patient's unconscious. As the therapist pushes to find more hidden memories, the client, who is already trained in the process, often comes up with still more accounts of having

been abused. . . . [Eventually,] the client's worst fears are forged into memories. What could be more psychologically damaging than being raped by one's father? Having to have his baby. What could be worse than having to give birth to your father's child? Having to kill the child. What could be worse than having to kill a baby? Having to eat the baby after you've killed it. What could be worse than all this? Having to do these things during ritualized worship of the Devil.

At such a juncture, readers may suppose, both parties to the "therapy" must surely awaken and realize that they have been taking a magic carpet ride. But for reasons that Ofshe and Watters supply, it doesn't happen. The therapist feels honor bound to avoid "revictimizing" the patient by expressing doubts, and the patient, precisely by virtue of having renounced the actual memories that used to moor her identity, has lost contact with reality and is desperate to retain the therapist's approval. The outcome is a potentially lethal *folie à deux*.

"If there are those who are unsure whether, or how, they were abused, . . . fully undertaking this course of committed introspection can only lead to greater honesty, gentleness, and openness."

Repressed Memory Therapy Helps Victims

Ruth Wallen

Authors and experts estimate that between 10 percent and 38 percent of girls are victims of sexual abuse. In the following viewpoint, Ruth Wallen asserts that healing from the effects of such abuse requires recovering memories that have been repressed and denied. She contends that the backlash against recovered memory therapy minimizes the problem of child sexual abuse. Wallen is a writer and teacher in San Diego, California.

As you read, consider the following questions:

1. How is the backlash against recovered memories reactionary in the worst sense, according to Wallen?
2. How does Carol Tavris, cited by the author, define healing? How does the author define healing?
3. How does Wallen describe disassociation?

Excerpted from Ruth Wallen, "Memory Politics: The Implications of Healing from Sexual Abuse." Reprinted from TIKKUN MAGAZINE, A BI-MONTHLY JEWISH CRITIQUE OF POLITICS, CULTURE, AND SOCIETY (November/December 1994). Subscriptions are $31/year from TIKKUN, 251 W. 100th St., 5th Fl., New York, NY 10025. Reproduced by permission of TIKKUN.

Over the last few years, I have made the harrowing journey common to many—remembering and speaking the truth about being sexually abused as a child. My vagina inexplicably burning, red, swollen, and itching. Nighttime seizures where my legs would part, my body curl and clench, and then begin to heave against my will. Suddenly understanding the lifelong mantra, "Don't touch me, don't touch me." Although I had often backpacked alone in the mountains, now I was too terrified to make art or write. Initially the panic was more palpable than any feelings of sadness or anger. I could work for a half-hour before I was reduced to a trembling child clutching at pillows, rocking, rocking, rocking. . . . My body was trying to remember.

Recovering from Remembered Abuse

As I learned to swim through the flood of memories, I wondered what else I'd forgotten or failed to notice. I never had illusions of an idyllic childhood and had always remembered some of my experience. Even so, I had often been so consumed in warding off my own pain, that I'd also chased away my dreams. Afraid of my own feelings, I had also shielded my heart from friends' grief and anger or used a distanced compassion to occlude the commonality of our feelings. As I learned to work with my panic, I felt tremendous energy, relief from no longer defending against a part of my experience. Less consumed with my own trauma, I remembered that outside my window there were mountains behind the dirty-brown southern California smog. I was not only interested in enriching forgotten corners of my private life, but also in sharing my understanding with others. I hoped that breaking the silence about the prevalence of sexual abuse would contribute to significant changes in society.

But my celebration of memory has been tempered by a recent shift in media coverage. Finally, I thought, people were daring to speak about the reality of sexual abuse. Almost every women's magazine covered sexual abuse, and Oprah Winfrey hosted a special on abuse of children on all three major networks. Yet instead of this coverage prompting further discussion about how to stop the frequent abuse of children, the existence of the problem itself is again the subject of debate.

The Backlash Against Recovered Memory

Accusations of false claims have dominated the news. As the story goes, bright, high-achieving white adults in their thirties or forties seek help for a minor life crisis, only to be convinced by an overzealous therapist that they've been horrifically abused in childhood. Or these same therapists, in cahoots with overly protective parents, con kids into thinking they're being molested. For example, the *Newsweek* cover of April 19, 1993, displayed the headline, "CHILD ABUSE," stamped across the sepia-toned faces of grandparents who had been convicted of abuse. The subheading conjured up "witch hunts" and asked, "When does the fight to protect our kids go too far?"

Post-Incest Syndrome Is Real

[The] argument that false memories of child abuse can be created by overzealous therapists is groundless. There is no evidence that anyone who was not sexually abused can be persuaded otherwise, let alone made to suffer post-incest syndrome.

How do I know that the majority of my clients are incest survivors, even when they almost never identify incest as their reason for seeking help? The terror and despair and self-hate and death wish that they struggle with on a daily basis tell me that something real, something horrible, was done to them. Their belief that sex is what you must pay back for love, the fact that all sex may feel like rape, indicate that the trauma was of a sexual nature. Their inability to trust or bond, their deep sense of loss, their belief that they are entitled to nothing in life tell me that the trauma was at the hands of someone with whom they had a dependency bond.

E. Sue Blume, the *New York Times Book Review*, February 14, 1993.

Much of the media coverage questioning the accuracy of memories about abuse has been fueled by conferences and press releases sponsored by the False Memory Syndrome Foundation, a group of a few thousand parents who claim that they have been falsely accused. It is significant that one of the lengthiest discussions of arguments promulgated by this foundation, in *Family Therapy Networker* (September/October 1993), mentions that four out of the five women who had retracted their charges of abuse and have become star witnesses for the group were in fact molested by someone. Despite this fact, when reporters cite these examples, they imply that charges of sexual abuse have been conjured up out of nowhere. Then the discussion typically focuses on supposed false accusations instead of the devastating fact of the abuse.

Stories of abuse have perhaps finally touched too close to home; maybe many middle-class Americans are not ready to believe that members of their communities could do such a thing to their own children. As if in reaction, public discussion has shifted to debate over the accuracy of memory. Whether intentional or reflexive, this backlash is reactionary in the worst sense, since it saps energy and attention from the question of how we can heal from the effects of abuse.

Healing from sexual abuse is profoundly empowering. But the process is slow, subtle, difficult, and unglamorous. In contrast, all of the recent articles that question the reality of sexual abuse focus on individual, sensational case histories rather than on the larger picture. Media coverage of this sort, while perhaps making for flashier headlines, encourages hysteria and a state of continued paralysis, effectively putting victims back in their place.

Trashing the Recovery Movement

The bashing of self-help books, the readiness of many detractors to dismiss the challenge of healing, is another manifestation of the backlash. While the critics accuse the survivor movement of oversimplification and overstatement, their contentions tend to be much more reductive than the self-help manuals they malign. Instead of recognizing the gravity of the problem, offering constructive suggestions, or discussing the complexity of the issues, these writers opt for the easier route of trashing recovery movements per se.

For instance, an article in January 1993 in the *New York Times Book Review* by Carol Tavris warns, "Beware the Incest-Survivor Machine." The piece lambastes the "incest survivor recovery movement" for its insularity, pop psychology, and claims that understanding past victimization will solve all current problems. While Tavris's claims that too often the broader social connections fail to be made is well-founded, instead of developing this argument, the bulk of the article indulges in a facile dismissal of self-help books. Tavris discounts the importance of sharing memories, reclaiming self-esteem, and kindling the courage to experience deep rage and grief. Certainly we should all be aware of the pitfall of using newfound awareness as better armor, instead of as a path toward greater openness. But Tavris and her fellow detractors fail to recognize that social responsibility must begin with self-reckoning and self-healing.

Articles such as Tavris's decry what they disdain as the incest survivor bandwagon. They scorn manuals for incest survivors, such as *The Courage to Heal*, by Ellen Bass and Laura Davis, for suggesting that one may be abused even if one has no specific memories, that if "you still have a feeling that something abusive happened to you, it probably did." But in the context in which this statement was written, it was meant to combat our cultural legacies of self-doubt and denial. Those who think they may have been abused and healing professionals must find a middle ground between believing that everyone who fits a generalized list of symptoms has been abused and, as in the past, repressing the very discussion of the abuse that these lists were meant to combat.

119

Undoubtedly, there are those who will grab at the latest explanation for all of life's woes. But detractors ought to recognize that for most survivors, acknowledging abuse is an extremely painful, disorienting, consuming experience that still carries with it great shame and trauma. It takes boundless compassion to learn to embrace a part of one's being that at first encounter feels so helpless, so wounded—and, from the therapist's perspective, to witness stories of intense suffering. It is extremely important, however, that the therapist, healer, or friend follow the survivor's lead during this process. If the survivor is in charge of the process, he or she is more likely to end up feeling empowered rather than duped. Even Bass and Davis condemn the "excesses" of the recovery movement. The therapist must be extremely careful about presuming that abuse is an explanation for current symptoms, asking leading questions, and suggesting what might have happened. Requiring clients with no memories to watch films and read books about abuse and using powerful drugs to recover memory are poor therapies.

I take strong issue with Tavris's claim that "healing is defined as your realization that you were a victim of sexual abuse and that it explains everything wrong in your life." The process of healing is precisely the eschewal of the victim identity and the acknowledgement of the ways in which one was unable to provide loving care for oneself and others. It cannot be repeated enough that, contrary to detractors' snide claims, genuine healing has nothing to do with justification of one's faults, or winning the badge of a survivor/victim. Healing involves an intense commitment to honesty with oneself, from the development of the strength to feel deep pain and rage, to learning to let go. . . .

The Prevalence of Sexual Abuse

The most conservative figures suggest that sexual abuse is rampant. The lowest estimate cited in *Newsweek* suggests that since the 1940s, 10 to 12 percent of girls under fourteen (unreasonably ignoring both boys and teenage abuse) have been sexually molested. Many writers estimate the figure is one girl in three and one boy in ten. Diana Russell's *The Secret Trauma* is the most frequently cited study. Analyzing interviews with 930 women in San Francisco, she found that 38 percent of women had been sexually abused (defined as "exploitive sexual contact or attempted contact") by the age of eighteen, 89 percent of these by relatives or family acquaintances. But even *Newsweek's* conservative estimate—one out of every nine or ten girls molested—is an outrageously unacceptable number.

Today, most of us know both victims and perpetrators. What is the impact on society of the tolerance of this behavior—an assault so intense, so intimate, that the victim can often only respond by amnesia, by splitting off from the wound? Alice Miller, a psychoanalyst and author of many books on child abuse, is the most eloquent spokesperson for the argument that until the victim can bear the truth, can release the secret held in the body, the trauma will be unconsciously reenacted, tormenting both self and others. Miller contends that children are especially vulnerable to abuse because they are frequently used to satisfy the narcissistic needs of their parents. The proliferation in our society of the means of destruction, from guns, to nuclear bombs, to environmental degradation, only escalates the urgency to turn our attention to ways to break the generational inheritance of violence.

Telling the Secret

At survivors' meetings I have attended, I have been most touched by hearing mothers grieve about having unwittingly passed on the cycle of abuse, of having been unable to nurture, love, or protect their children fully because they were too withdrawn, defended from their own pain. Breaking this cycle begins with the courage to be vulnerable, to move into the tightly held energy, the secret places, without any certainty about what will emerge. And if there are those who are unsure whether, or how, they were abused, but feel that they have these wounds to heal, fully undertaking this course of committed introspection can only lead to greater honesty, gentleness, and openness. The initial stages of healing involve introspection, not accusation. Thus, the healing process can serve as an inspiration to all who suffer from disassociative trauma.

The incest victim has mastered the art of disassociation, secrecy, and denial. Pain felt by the body has been called pleasure. Violation has been called love. When the body has actually felt pleasure, or the heart love, mind has felt betrayed, deeply ashamed for having failed to fully resist the encounter. Pummeled by the logic of double-speak, intellect has learned to resist any sensation, distrust all feelings. Mind has been split from body has been severed from heart. "Never tell" is the mantra. Over and over, this threat has been repeated: Something terrible will happen if the secret is revealed. Even worse than the distortion of the parental bond is the denial of intimacy with oneself. Honesty has been replaced with tremendous fear, distrust, and even loathing of one's secret, dark experience. And this secret festers, feeding on the ambiguity and silence, coiling inward as a dagger of self-deprecation.

It is not the abuse itself as much as the acceptance of the perpetrator's admonishment not to tell that is so crippling. In keeping the secret, one is forced to construct a rigid identity that insulates oneself from hidden pain. One perpetuates the abuse by rejecting a part of oneself. The constant struggle to repel pain becomes a habit hard to break, extending beyond the abusive trauma, to all direct experience.

Daring to touch the wound, embracing the "bad girl," is a radical move. After the initial shock, healing is a slow process of realignment of severed connections and reestablishment of circulation. As one's heart is cracked open by experiencing the depth of trauma, the confidence engendered by experiencing the emotion, releasing the energy, moves one beyond the sense of helpless victimization. Slowly, the prohibition against experiencing one's innermost secrets is dissolved. The release of the emotion at the core of the violation turns out not to be so terrifying, or painful, as the years of avoidance and resistance. Speaking the truth can be profoundly liberating. One is no longer at war with oneself. Pandora's box turns out to be a myth invented by the perpetrator, a terribly pernicious myth that preserves self-loathing and keeps one not only from remembering the past, but from fully experiencing the present. Developing the courage to cease censoring feelings and to name experience honestly, while a slow process, is tremendously empowering. And although the change may initially be unsettling for close friends and family, it ultimately serves as an invitation to all to examine and heal destructive relationships, as well as the secret, discarded aspects of ourselves. . . .

At the current moment, many people are quick to dismiss the testimonials of sexual abuse as a passing fad, perhaps impelled by the urge to raise doubt before the victim's voices have had time to make connections or to recognize the patterns that go beyond their individual experience. I am slowly coming to the realization that however much I remember, I will never know every detail, never know exactly what happened. A part of me will always shudder in disbelief. But despite external pressures, I need not choose the powerlessness of self-doubt or victimhood. Together with other survivors, I can share my broken heart. Together, we can feel our grief and rage and not shy away from naming our experience. Contrary to what we have been told, something terrible will happen if the secret is not shared.

"[The mission of talk shows] is not to get beneath our assumptions and stereotypes but to exploit and solidify them."

Talk Shows Exploit Society's Victims

Jill Nelson

Daytime talk show hosts such as Oprah Winfrey defend their programs as a forum for examining a wide range of psychological, social, and sexual issues. In the following viewpoint, Jill Nelson argues that talk shows reduce these issues to a form of entertainment based on the humiliation of guests, a process that kills any compassion among viewers for those with problems. Rather than creating understanding among people, Nelson contends, these shows perpetuate the worst stereotypes. Nelson is the author of *Volunteer Slavery: My Authentic Negro Experience*.

As you read, consider the following questions:

1. According to Nelson, what are the cornerstones of Oprah Winfrey's success?
2. What does the author find more terrifying than the killing of talk show guest Scott Amedure?
3. What is the typical format of a talk show, according to the author?

Jill Nelson, "Talk Is Cheap," *Nation*, June 5, 1995. Reprinted with permission from the *Nation* magazine; © The Nation Company, L.P.

On a plane headed to New York, my seatmate is a young woman who confides that she is on her way to be a guest on *Rolonda*, one of dozens of syndicated talk shows currently on television. "What's the topic?" I ask.

"Secret crushes."

"Do you have one?" I wonder. By the time we land in New York, I find out she doesn't, though she's told the producers she does and given them the name of a man she vaguely knows. It turns out that she and her girlfriends were sitting around watching *Rolonda*, and when the call for guests with secret crushes came up during a break, complete with an 800 number, she picked up the phone as a goof. Except *Rolonda*'s producers didn't know it was a joke, or didn't care. She says they called her more than ten times, and in exchange for airfare, a hotel room and a limo, she's agreed to risk public humiliation. The producers even suggested she bring a pair of panties as a gift for her crush, but she drew the line. She did agree to lug a suitcase full of local gourmet specialties for them.

Over the course of a few months I spent several hours a day, five days a week, watching talk shows. From Rolonda to Geraldo to Jenny Jones to Richard Bey to Donahue to Ricki Lake to Gordon Elliott to Jerry Springer to Sally Jessy Raphael to Maury Povich to Montel Williams to Oprah. I've watched shows on mate swapping, men who beat women, fat women who are porno stars, the superiority in size of black men's penises, transvestites, men who don't support their children, bisexuality, people who love to have unprotected sex, women who love murderers, children who are out of control, white women who love black men, strippers, black women who love white men. You name it, I've probably seen it; I've seen it all.

The Rise of Victim-Oriented Talk Shows

In 1986, when *The Oprah Winfrey Show* went national, media attention focused on what impact Winfrey's personal, emotional style would have on the ratings of the longtime king of serious daytime talk, Phil Donahue. Television critics grumbled that her confessional approach—and soaring ratings—would force the news-oriented Donahue to abandon his format. Almost a decade later, it's clear that Winfrey's success influenced a lot more than Phil Donahue. Imitators have taken the cornerstones of Winfrey's success—guests who confess their victimization, confront their victimizer, and through public confession hope for some sort of healing—and reduced it to its lowest common denominator. They've taken Winfrey's formula to its most hideous extreme, leaving Winfrey, who is appalled by what she created (in 1994 she announced she would change her format), and Donahue, who always seemed uncomfortable with the role of priest in TV's confessional, seeming to be above it all. Today's talk shows celebrate victim and victimizer equally; they draw no lines and have no values except the almighty dollar. And, cheap as they are to produce, they pay: Over the past decade [since 1986], television talk shows have proliferated like roaches in the walls of a New York City apartment building.

Reprinted by permission: Tribune Media Services.

In a fundamental way, the success of these shows is based on external economic, social and political factors: the disappearance of entry-level employment for young high school graduates, the disintegration of communities, the elimination of government support programs for young people and families—from school loans to daycare centers to community-based health facilities—and the resulting despair and rage that pervade many people's lives. Like the woman on the airplane, they crave their fifteen minutes of fame, with its illusion of success and importance. An appearance on television, even if it is based on a lie and depends upon making themselves and others look ridiculous, is their best chance of attaining it. The audience too, both in the studio and at home, feeds off the misery and humiliation of others. Less obvious is the price we all pay for those fifteen minutes in increased alienation, contempt and hatred.

The current crop of talk shows exists solely as entertainment based on the humiliation, or potential humiliation, of their

125

guests. Much has been made of the March 1995 murder of a gay man, Scott Amedure. Jonathan Schmitz, apparently unable to stand the thought of being desired by another man, shot and killed Amedure several days after he confessed at a taping of the *Jenny Jones* show that Schmitz was his "secret crush." But as frightening as that was, I'm more terrified by the daily killing off of any sense of understanding, connectedness, collective responsibility and the potential for redemption that these talk shows foster.

The effect is subtle, cumulative and wholly negative. With the frequent exception of Donahue, and occasionally Oprah, I cannot say that I learned one useful thing, gained any understanding or was ever informed or enriched after months of watching Ricki, Montel, Richard Bey and the rest of the crew. For the first few days I found the programs amusing, in a snide way. It was initially fascinating to watch people spill the most intimate details about their sex lives, lack of value systems, antisocial activities and absence of a connection to a community greater than the self. But after the first week, I was embarrassed, sickened and enraged by what I heard.

I found myself yearning for the good old days of talk shows hosted by the likes of Joe Pyne, Alan Burke and Morton Downey Jr., who made their own prejudices and politics so clear that they provided a contrast to their guests, a line of demarcation around which sides could be taken. Today's talk-show hosts are slick media creations masquerading as people like us: hip Ricki, macho ex-Marine Montel, middle-aged, clean-cut suburban types à la Jenny Jones, Jerry Springer and Maury Povich. Where Pyne, Burke and Downey were full of opinions and vitriol, these hosts pose as facilitators, egging their guests on to greater revelation and humiliation while they remain above the fray, inquiring minds who want to know.

Everyone Is a Stereotype

But their mission is not to get beneath our assumptions and stereotypes but to exploit and solidify them. The guests are overwhelmingly young, mostly black and Latino, apparently poor and often unemployed. Their personalities and behaviors are cast as representative. Young black men become walking penises. Young women of all colors are victims; or stupid, sex-addicted, dependent baby-makers, with an occasional castrating bitch thrown in. Young white males are either nerds or, to the extent they are able to mimic the antisocial, highly sexualized behavior of the black males, equally obnoxious, dick-identified studs.

In the world of talk, young black men are portrayed as arrogant, amoral, violent predators out to get you with their penis, their gun or both. A few pathological individuals are presented as representatives of the group, and there's seldom any discussion of the economic, social and political conditions that produce antisocial behavior. It's hard to recall seeing any young black man on TV representing the majority: decent guys struggling to get a foothold in a society that provides scant support and expects the worst. You'd think that when the first-grade teacher asked the class what they wanted to do when they grew up, all the black boys raised their hands and said, "Deal crack, decimate my community and do drive-bys."

This representation of black men as dicks is the dominant motif of many of the shows: "I wouldn't sleep with him so he dumped me," "My man's a dog and you can have him," "Confronting the person who dumped you," "Women who let their men have sex with other women," "I'd do anything for my man" and endless variations of "secret crush," "dating game" and "he has to choose between me and her."

An Unvarying Format

Whatever the topic, the format is as follows: One person—usually a woman, since women are most frequently cast in the role of stupid, powerless victim—comes out and tells all the couple's business to the apparently sympathetic host and a leering, jeering, cheering audience of her peers. This done, the other person—usually a man—is brought onstage, where he is confronted by his woman/women, booed or cheered by the audience, and gleefully encouraged by the host to confirm our worst suspicions. It was initially interesting to see that a significant number of these couples are interracial, but the subtext quickly became clear: Penis-waving black men prey not only on black women, who deserve/are used to it, but on WHITE WOMEN. Thus the shows confirm the popular political line that black men are to be feared—not only in the street but in the bedroom. Violence, teenage pregnancy, poverty, spousal abuse, the spread of AIDS and other sexually transmitted diseases, Aid to Families with Dependent Children (A.F.D.C.)—you name it and Mandingo's behind it.

Unfortunately, TV's Mandingo seldom disappoints. Neither does young Mr. Charlie. This is not surprising, since the desperate desire to be seen, recognized and on TV appears to have overriden 95 percent of whatever common sense exists. Almost daily, I witnessed a man attacked for his sexual promiscuity stand up and proudly gyrate or clutch his penis for the camera. I began to wonder if talk-show producers' pre-interview of prospective guests consists of anything more than asking them to execute a bump and grind.

It's rare that guests are given any advice, analysis or support.

127

There is almost never a psychologist, counselor or even a writer hawking a book on the topic to listen, place in context or advise remedial action. A few talk shows use audience members as counselors or judges, but this is solely for entertainment value. The guests have gotten their fifteen minutes of fame, but leave essentially as they came: alienated, angry and, most important, jobless. The hosts leave with a fat paycheck.

The Effect of Talk Shows

All this has a profound political effect; daytime talk shows, intentionally or not, have become storm troopers for the right. Both the talk shows and the right wing erase the line between the anecdotal and the factual. Both focus attention on the individual, aberrant behavior of a small number of citizens and declare them representative of a group. So the black woman labeled a "welfare cheat" by elected officials comes to represent *most* women receiving Aid to Families with Dependent Children, when the overwhelming majority of women receiving A.F.D.C. do not "cheat" the system and would like nothing better than to get a job with benefits greater than those provided by welfare. Rather than present an honest look at what life on welfare's really like and initiating a discussion of positive "welfare reform," most talk shows seek out the exception who appears to prove the right-wing rule: a poor, uneducated, twenty-one-year-old woman on welfare with four children. Why bother to have a serious discussion about education, unemployment or building community when it's so much easier to demonize poor black women?

Watching TV talk shows was like being caught in a daylong downpour of fear, hostility and paranoia. I found myself feeling meanspirited and snarling by the time the news came on at 6 o'clock, and full of lust for revenge. In that mood it was almost possible to entertain the notion that old Newt Gingrich might have some good ideas. Maybe we ought to take out a Contract with America and punish the young, poor, female, black, Latino and gay—those troublemakers we've watched swagger through talk shows all day.

While the pundits and President Bill Clinton discuss the negative impact of right-wing radio talk shows in the wake of the Oklahoma bombing, TV talk continues unnoticed and unanalyzed. But television reaches a much broader audience than the already converted who tune in to talk-radio. Television gives not only a voice but a face to our fear and rage, enables us to point the finger of blame at the tube—at "them"—and roar for punishment. Isn't that what the Contract with America is all about?

"For people whose desires and identities go against the norm, [talk shows are] the only spot in mainstream media culture to speak on our own terms."

Talk Shows Give a Forum to Society's Victims

Joshua Gamson

Daytime talk shows have been maligned by media critics as "freak shows" that exploit people with psychological problems without providing them any counseling or therapeutic benefit. In the following viewpoint, Joshua Gamson maintains that even if daytime programs are freak shows, they provide a rare forum where those labeled freaks—especially nonheterosexuals—are given visibility and support and a chance to speak out. Gamson is assistant professor of sociology at Yale University in New Haven, Connecticut, and author of *Claims to Fame: Celebrity in Contemporary America*.

As you read, consider the following questions:

1. According to Gamson's account, how were antigay guests denounced on the *Ricki Lake* show?
2. What fact was glossed over in reports of the murder of talk show guest Scott Amedure, according to the author?
3. What does the author say is the second voice promoted by the talk show?

Joshua Gamson, "Do Ask, Do Tell: Freak Talk on TV." Reprinted with permission from the *American Prospect*, Fall 1995; © New Prospect, Inc.

For lesbians, gay men, bisexuals, drag queens, or transsexuals, or some combination thereof, watching daytime television has got to be spooky. Suddenly, there are renditions of you, chattering away in a system that otherwise ignores or steals your voice at every turn. Sally Jessy Raphael wants to know what it's like to pass as a different sex, Phil Donahue wants to support you in your battle against gay bashing, Ricki Lake wants to get you a date, Oprah Winfrey wants you to love without lying. Most of all, they all want you to talk about it publicly, just at a time when everyone else wants you not to. They are interested, if not precisely in "reality," at least not (with possible exceptions) in fictional accounts. For people whose desires and identities go against the norm, this is the only spot in mainstream media culture to speak on our own terms or to hear others speaking for themselves. The fact that it is so much maligned, and for so many good reasons, does not close the case.

Daytime Exposure

I happened to turn on the *Ricki Lake Show*, for example, which, as the fastest rising talk show ever, has quickly reached first place among its target audience of eighteen-to-thirty-four-year-old women. The topic: "I don't want gays around my kids." I caught the last twenty minutes of what amounted to a pro-gay screamfest. Ricki and her audience explicitly attacked a large woman who was denying visitation rights to her gay ex-husband ("I had to explain to a nine-year-old what 'gay' means," and "My child started having nightmares after he visited his father"). And they went at a young couple who believed in keeping children away from gay people on the grounds that the Bible says "homosexuals should die." The gay guests and their supporters had the last word, brought on to argue, to much audience whooping, that loving gays are a positive influence and hateful heterosexuals should stay away from children. The antigay guests were denounced on any number of grounds, by host, other guests, and numerous audience members: They are denying children loving influences, they are bigots, they are misinformed, they read the Bible incorrectly, they sound like Mormons, they are resentful that they have put on more weight than their exes. One suburban-looking audience member angrily addressed each "child protector" in turn, along the way coming up with my new favorite apostrophe, and possible new pageant theme, as she lit into a blue-dressed woman: "And as for you, Miss Homophobia. . . ."

The show was a typical mess, with guests yelling and audiences hooting at the best one-liners about bigotry or body weight, but the virulence with which homophobia was attacked is both typical of these shows and stunning. When Ms. Lake cut off a long-sideburned man's argument that "it's a fact that the easiest way to get AIDS is by homosexual sex" ("That is not a fact, sir, that is not correct"), I found myself ready to start the chant of "Go, Ricki! Go, Ricki!" that apparently wraps each taping. Even such elementary corrections, and even such a weird form of visibility and support, stands out sharply. Here, the homophobe is the deviant, the freak. . . .

This Side of a Fistfight

While they highlight different sex and gender identities, expressions, and practices, the talk shows can be a dangerous place to speak and a difficult place to get heard. With around twenty syndicated talk shows competing for audiences, shows that trade in confrontation and surprise (*Ricki Lake, Jenny Jones, Jerry Springer*) are edging out the milder, topical programs (*Oprah, Donahue*). Although Winfrey is still number one, with an estimated 9.4 million viewers, her ratings have declined significantly. Unquestionably, "exploitalk" is winning out, and the prize is big: A successful talk show, relatively cheap to produce, can reportedly make more than $50 million a year in profits.

One way to the prize, the "ambush" of guests with surprises, is fast becoming a talk show staple. As Ricki Lake, whose show reaches an estimated audience of 5.8 million, told a reporter, the ambush "does so much for the energy of the show." Even without an ambush, a former *Jane Whitney Show* producer told *TV Guide*, "When you're booking guests, you're thinking, 'How much confrontation can this person provide me?' The more confrontation, the better. You want people just this side of a fistfight."

Violence on the Talk Shows

For members of groups already subject to violence, the visibility of television can prompt more than just a fistfight, as the *Jenny Jones* murder underlined. In March 1995, when Scott Amedure appeared on a "secret admirer" episode of the *Jenny Jones Show* (currently number three in the national syndicated talk show ratings), the admired Jonathan Schmitz was apparently expecting a female admirer. Schmitz, not warming to Amedure's fantasy of tying him up in a hammock and spraying whipped cream and champagne on his body, declared himself "100 percent heterosexual." Later, back in Michigan, he punctuated this claim by shooting Amedure with a 12-gauge shotgun, telling police that the embarrassment from the program had "eaten away" at him. Or, as he reportedly put it in his 911 call, Amedure "fucked me on national TV."

Critics were quick to point out that programming that creates conflict tends to exacerbate it. "The producers made professions of regret," cultural critic Neal Gabler wrote in the *Los Angeles Times* after the Amedure murder, "but one suspects what they really regretted was the killer's indecency of not having pulled out his rifle and committed the crime before their cameras." In the wake of the murder, talk show producers were likened over and over to drug dealers: Publicist Ken Maley told the *San Francisco Chronicle* that "they've got people strung out on an adrenaline rush," and "they keep raising the dosage"; sociologist Vicki Abt told *People* that "TV allows us to mainline deviance"; Michelangelo Signorile argued in *Out* that some talk show producers "are like crack dealers scouring trailer park America." True enough. Entering the unruly talk show world one tends to become, at best, a source of adrenaline rush, and at worst a target of violence.

The Oprah Winfrey Show Helps People

When viewers around the world tune in each weekday to watch *The Oprah Winfrey Show*, it's a sure bet that somebody, somewhere is going to benefit from the day's topic.

Whether it's a show on finding lost loved ones, creating a loving environment in a stepfamily or lifesaving first aid techniques, *The Oprah Winfrey Show* helps people live better lives.

Trudy Moore, *Jet*, April 18, 1994.

What most reporting tended to gloss, however, was that most antigay violence does not require a talk show "ambush" to trigger it. Like the Oakland County, Michigan, prosecutor, who argued that "*Jenny Jones*'s producers' cynical pursuit of ratings and total insensitivity to what could occur here left one person dead and Mr. Schmitz now facing life in prison," many critics focused on the "humiliating" surprise attack on Schmitz with the news that he was desired by another man. As in the image of the "straight" soldier being ogled in the shower, in this logic the revelation of same-sex desire is treated as the danger, and the desired as a victim. The talk show critics thus played to the same "don't tell" logic that makes talk shows such a necessary, if uncomfortable, refuge for some of us.

Although producers' pursuit of ratings is indeed, unsurprisingly, cynical and insensitive, the talk show environment is one of the very few in which the declaration of same-sex desire (and, to a lesser degree, atypical gender identity) is common, heartily defended, and often even incidental. Although they overlook this in their haste to hate trash, the critics of exploitative talk shows help illuminate the odd sort of opportunity these cacophonous settings provide. Same-sex desires become "normalized" on these programs not so much because different sorts of lives become clearly visible, but because they get sucked into the spectacular whirlpool of relationship conflicts. They offer a particular kind of visibility and voice. On *Ricki Lake*, it was the voice of an aggressive, screechy gay man who continually reminded viewers, between laughing at his own nasty comments, that he was a regular guy. On other days, it's the take-your-hands-off-my-woman lesbian, or the I'm-more-of-a-woman-than-you'll-ever-be transsexual. Here is the first voice talk shows promote, one price of entry into mainstream public visibility: the vicious one, shouting that we gay people can be as mean, or petty, or just plain loud, as anybody else.

Spectacle and Conversation

The guests on the talk shows seem to march in what psychologist Jeanne Heaton, coauthor of *Tuning in Trouble*, calls a "parade of pathology." Many talk shows have more than a passing resemblance to freak shows. Neal Gabler, for example, argues that guests are invited to exhibit "their deformities for attention" in a "ritual of debasement" aimed primarily at reassuring the audience of its superiority. Indeed, the evidence for dehumanization is all over the place, especially when it comes to gender crossing, as in the titles of various recent *Geraldo* programs, in which the calls of sideshow barkers echo: "Star-crossed crossdressers: bizarre stories of transvestites and their lovers," and "Outrageous impersonators and flamboyant drag queens," and "When your husband wears the dress in the family," and "Girly to burly: women who became men." As long as talk shows make their bids by being, in Gabler's words, "a psychological freak show," sex and gender outsiders entering them arguably reinforce their inhuman, outsider status, by entering a discourse in which they are bizarre, outrageous, flamboyant curiosities. (Often when they do this, for example, they must relinquish their right to define themselves to the ubiquitous talk show "experts.")

Talk shows do indeed trade on voyeurism, and it is no secret that those who break with sex and gender norms and fight with each other on camera help the shows win higher ratings. But there is more to the picture. This is the place where "freaks" talk back. It is a place where Conrad, born and living in a female body, can assert against Sally Jessy Raphael's claims that he "used and betrayed" women in order to have sex with them, that women fall in love with him as a man because he considers himself a man; where months later, in a program on "our most outrageous former guests" (all gender crossers), Conrad can reappear, declare himself to have started hormone treatment, and report that the woman he allegedly "used and betrayed" has stood by him. This is a narrow opening, but an opening nonetheless, for the second voice promoted by the talk show: the proud voice of the "freak," even if the freak refuses that term. The fact that talk shows are exploitative spectacles does not negate the fact that they are also opportunities; as media scholar Wayne Munson points out, they are both spectacle and conversation. They give voice to those systematically silenced, albeit under conditions out of the speaker's control, and in voices that come out tinny, scratched, distant.

Periodical Bibliography

The following articles have been selected to supplement the diverse views presented in this chapter. Addresses are provided for periodicals not indexed in the *Readers' Guide to Periodical Literature,* the *Alternative Press Index,* or the *Social Sciences Index.*

Melinda Blau	"Recovery Fever," *New York,* September 9, 1991.
Michael Brennan	"Self-Indulgent Self-Help," *Newsweek,* January 20, 1992.
Andrew Delbanco and Thomas Delbanco	"A.A. at the Crossroads," *New Yorker,* March 20, 1995.
John Fowler	"The Troubling World of Recovered Memory," *World & I,* December 1994. Available from 3600 New York Ave. NE, Washington, DC 20002.
Maryanne Garry and Elizabeth F. Loftus	"Repressed Memories of Childhood Trauma: Could Some of Them Be Suggested?" *USA Today,* January 1994.
Mark G. Judge	"Diagnosed Alcoholic," *Sojourners,* August/September 1992.
Dana Mack	"Are Parents Bad for Children?" *Commentary,* March 1994.
Elizabeth M. Matz	"When Backlash Causes Whiplash: The Media Blitz of Victim Blaming," *Off Our Backs,* November 1994.
Paul R. McHugh	"Psychotherapy Awry," *American Scholar,* Winter 1994.
Richard Ofshe and Ethan Watters	"Making Monsters," *Society,* March/April 1993.
Charles Oliver	"Freak Parade," *Reason,* April 1995.
Elayne Rapping	"Needed: A Radical Recovery," *Progressive,* January 1993.
Ruth Shalit	"Witch Hunt," *New Republic,* June 19, 1995.
Laura Shapiro	"Rush to Judgment," *Newsweek,* April 19, 1993.
Carol Tavris	"Beware the Incest-Survivor Machine," *New York Times Book Review,* January 3, 1993.
John Taylor	"The Lost Daughter," *Esquire,* March 1994.
Jane Whitney	"When Talk Gets Too Cheap," *U.S. News & World Report,* June 12, 1995.

4 CHAPTER

How Does "Victimhood" Affect the Justice System?

AMERICA'S VICTIMS

Chapter Preface

In February 1992, eighty-one-year-old Stella Liebeck purchased a cup of coffee from a McDonald's drive-through in Albuquerque, New Mexico. While taking the lid off the cup to add cream and sugar, she accidentally spilled the hot coffee in her lap. Because the coffee was heated to nearly 180 degrees, Liebeck received second- and third-degree burns and had to be hospitalized for a week. She subsequently filed a lawsuit against McDonald's Corporation, and in August 1994 a jury awarded Liebeck $160,000 in compensatory damages and $2.7 million in punitive damages (although the judge later reduced the total sum to $480,000).

Critics of the legal system point to this case to argue that jury awards in tort (personal injury) cases have become a lottery, awarding outrageous sums to irresponsible "victims" who do harm to themselves but blame someone else. *U.S. News & World Report* columnist John Leo, who is a vocal critic of the tort system, argues that too many Americans hold the attitude that "everything bad that happens to us is someone else's fault, and someone else must be made to pay." Liebeck, for instance, spilled the coffee on herself as she sat in a car trying to balance the cup on her knee, critics point out. They claim the $2.7 million award was excessively punitive toward McDonald's for an accident that it did not cause (as the judge apparently decided).

Others maintain that the tort system is effective in punishing corporations that negligently cause harm to individuals. In the case of McDonald's coffee, Charles Allen, Liebeck's son-in-law, says, "The system worked as it was supposed to." McDonald's heated its coffee to a temperature that would cause third-degree burns, he points out, and evidence presented at the trial showed that McDonald's was aware of the problem but did nothing to remedy it. He argues that the $2.7 million judgment handed down by the jury sent a message to McDonald's to act more responsibly. "The reasonable jury told this irresponsible corporation that its behavior was unacceptable," according to Allen.

From claims of irresponsibility in tort cases to so-called abuse excuses in criminal trials, the viewpoints in the following chapter debate the effects of victimhood on the justice system.

"More and more defense lawyers are employing [the 'abuse excuse'] and more and more jurors are buying it."

The "Abuse Excuse" Is Detrimental to the Justice System

Alan M. Dershowitz

In a few highly publicized trials, such as the 1993–94 trial of Erik and Lyle Menendez for the murder of their parents, defendants have claimed that a history of abuse at the hands of their victims propelled them to retaliate violently. In the following viewpoint, Alan M. Dershowitz argues that this "abuse excuse" defense is dangerous because it enables people to abdicate responsibility for their actions, it legitimizes vigilantism, and it undermines faith in the criminal justice system. He contends that there is no scientific validity to such defenses, despite the fact that they have been validated in jurors' minds by daytime talk shows. Dershowitz is a criminal-defense attorney and author of *The Abuse Excuse*, from which this viewpoint is excerpted.

As you read, consider the following questions:

1. How does the author define the "abuse excuse"?
2. What is the old-fashioned form of vigilantism, according to Dershowitz? What is the new-fashioned form?
3. What is the basic fallacy underlying each form of the abuse excuse, in the author's words?

The "abuse excuse"—the legal tactic by which criminal defendants claim a history of abuse as an excuse for violent retaliation—is quickly becoming a license to kill and maim. More and more defense lawyers are employing this tactic and more and more jurors are buying it. It is a dangerous trend, with serious and widespread implications for the safety and liberty of every American.

Among the recent excuses that have been accepted by at least some jurors have been "battered woman syndrome," "abused child syndrome," "rape trauma syndrome," and "urban survival syndrome." This has encouraged lawyers to try other abuse excuses, such as "black rage." For example, the defense lawyer for Colin Ferguson—the black man convicted in March 1995 of killing white commuters on the Long Island Railroad on December 7, 1993—has acknowledged that his black rage variation on the insanity defense "is similar to the utilization of the battered woman's syndrome, the post-traumatic stress syndrome and the child abuse syndrome in other cases to negate criminal accountability."

The Danger of Vigilantism

On the surface, the abuse excuse affects only the few handfuls of defendants who raise it, and those who are most immediately impacted by an acquittal or reduced charge. But at a deeper level, the abuse excuse is a symptom of a general abdication of responsibility by individuals, families, groups, and even nations. Its widespread acceptance is dangerous to the very tenets of democracy, which presuppose personal accountability for choices and actions. It also endangers our collective safety by legitimating a sense of vigilantism that reflects our frustration over the apparent inability of law enforcement to reduce the rampant violence that engulfs us.

At a time of ever-hardening attitudes toward crime and punishment, it may seem anomalous that so many jurors—indeed, so many Americans—appear to be sympathetic to the abuse excuse. But it is not anomalous at all, since the abuse excuse is a modern-day form of vigilantism—a recognition that since official law enforcement does not seem able to prevent or punish abuse, the victim should be entitled to take the law into his or her own hands.

In philosophical terms, the claim is that society has broken its "social contract" with the abused victim by not according him or her adequate protection. Because it has broken that social contract, the victim has been returned to a "state of nature" in which "might makes right" and the victim is entitled to invoke the law of the jungle—"kill or be killed." Indeed, these very terms were used in a 1994 Texas case in which one black youth

[Daimion Osby] killed two other blacks in a dangerous urban neighborhood. The result was a hung jury.

But vigilantism—whether it takes the old-fashioned form of the lynch mob or the new-fashioned form of the abuse victim's killing her sleeping husband—threatens the very fabric of our democracy and sows the seeds of anarchy and autocracy. The abuse excuse is dangerous, therefore, both in its narrow manifestation as a legal defense and in its broader manifestation as an abrogation of societal responsibility.

Affirmative Action in the Justice System

The other characteristic shared by these defenses is that they are often "politically correct," thus reflecting current trends toward employing different criteria of culpability when judging disadvantaged groups. In effect, these abuse excuse defenses, by emphasizing historical discrimination suffered by particular groups, seek to introduce some degree of affirmative action into our criminal-justice system.

Not Their Fault?

The most terrifying aspect of this latest version of the American dream is not that we are entitled to everything, but that we are responsible for nothing. That the juries could not reach a verdict in the Menendez cases [Erik and Lyle Menendez were accused of killing their parents], slapped the wrist of Damian Williams [convicted of "mayhem" for attacking trucker Reginald Denny during the 1992 Los Angeles riots], and allowed Lorena Bobbitt to walk [after she cut off her husband's penis], and did so in each case because the victimizers were perceived to have suffered, means that we have reached a new standard. We are entitled not just to the pursuit of happiness but to happiness itself. Any mild trauma, much less abuse, excuses any action, no matter how heinous. The twin mantras of the late twentieth century have become "I deserve better" and "It's not my fault."

Julia Reed, *Vogue*, May 1994.

These abuse-excuse defenses are the daily fare of the proliferating menu of TV and radio talk shows. It is virtually impossible to flip the TV channels during the daytime hours without seeing a bevy of sobbing women and men justifying their failed lives by reference to some past abuse, real or imagined. Personal responsibility does not sell soap as well as sob stories. Jurors who watch this stuff begin to believe it, despite its status as junk science. The very fact that Sally Jessy Raphael and Montel Williams repeat it as if it were gospel tends to legitimate it in the minds of some jurors. They are thus receptive to it in the courtroom, especially when the defendant is portrayed as sympathetic, and his dead victim is unsympathetic. William Kunstler is quick to point to public-opinion polls that show that "two-thirds of blacks and almost half the whites surveyed recognize the validity of our [black rage] theory of Mr. Ferguson's defense."

Most Victims Do Not Commit Violence

But neither public-opinion polls nor TV talk shows establish the empirical or normative validity of such abuse-excuse defenses. The basic fallacy underlying each of them is that the vast majority of people who have experienced abuses—whether it be sexual, racial, or anything else—do not commit violent crimes. Thus the abuse excuse neither explains nor justifies the violence. A history of abuse is not a psychological or a legal license to kill. It may, in some instances, be relevant at sentencing, but certainly not always.

Lest it be thought that the abuse excuse is credited only by radical defense lawyers, lay jurors, and talk-show-watching stay-at-homes, a quotation from the attorney general of the United States illustrates how pervasive this sort of thinking is becoming. In April 1993, Janet Reno was quoted as commenting on urban riots as follows: "An angry young man who lashes out in violence because he never had a childhood might do the right thing," and when the "right thing" is in contradiction with the law, "you try to get the law changed." I wonder if the angry young man's innocent victim agrees that the violence directed against his shop was the "right thing" and that the law protecting his property should be "changed."

The worst consequence of these abuse excuses is that they stigmatize all abuse victims with the violence of the very few who have used their victimization as a justification to kill or maim. The vast majority of abuse victims are neither prone to violence nor to making excuses.

"*Gender bias influences the way we perceive crime, criminal responsibility and justice.*"

The Abuse Defense Balances the Justice System

Leslie Abramson

In August 1989, Lyle and Erik Menendez killed their parents. At their 1993–94 trial, they claimed that the physical and sexual abuse they suffered at the hands of their father drove them to commit the killings in self-defense. In the following viewpoint, Los Angeles, California, criminal-defense attorney Leslie Abramson, who represented the Menendez brothers, contends that there has long been a double standard in the criminal justice system that accepts the violence of men but condemns violent acts committed by women or children in self-defense. She argues that the psychological effects of chronic abuse—the suffering and terror it engenders—often explain victims' violent retaliation against abusers and should therefore be accepted as a valid defense.

As you read, consider the following questions:

1. According to Abramson, what does the term "Texas Justice" describe?
2. According to the author, what are the forces that drive victims of abuse to act against their abusers?
3. What makes community support for O.J. Simpson troubling, in the author's opinion?

I never learned about "male justice" in school.

During my education in the New York City public schools, the City University of New York and the University of California, Los Angeles, School of Law, I was taught the noble fictions of our justice system. I was told that American justice is equal for all. I was instructed that the accused always is presumed innocent until proven guilty, and that the prosecution bears the burden of proving that guilt beyond a reasonable doubt.

By the end of my first year of practice I also had learned that much of what I'd been taught was naive. Most important, I discovered that the racism and sexism deforming so many of our institutions also infect the courts, producing a double standard of justice.

Much has been written about racism's insidious role in our criminal-justice system. But the recent cases of O.J. Simpson [acquitted of murder in October 1995], Lyle and Erik Mencndez [charged with murdering their parents, their trial resulted in hung juries in January 1994], and Lorena Bobbitt [acquitted of maiming her husband in January 1994] have opened a public debate on how gender bias influences the way we perceive crime, criminal responsibility and justice.

Justice for "Wronged" Men and Abused Women

"Texas Justice" was what we criminal lawyers used to call cases in which a man was acquitted after killing his wife and her lover *in flagrante delicto*. It mattered not if the victims were unarmed or asleep when the "wronged" man blew them away in his fit of jealous rage. No one went to the talk shows to decry the "heat of passion" defense employed by men expressing their possessory rights over the women of their choice—including the right to kill. Of course, no such right to kill was expressly provided in the written law, but the unwritten law—what might be called the male bill of rights—was implicitly understood by sympathetic male jurors.

The law of macho, of course, does not extend to women and children who kill. They rarely kill, but when they do, they don't do it out of wounded pride or from affronts to their sexuality or in the anger of the rejected. The forces that drive them to act are fear and terror, the motivations of the weak, the oppressed, the tortured and the broken. And they are scorned and ridiculed and hated for it.

We guiltily admire the successful barroom brawler, the fastest gun, the aggressive forechecker, the crushing lineman. The law of self-defense as currently codified in most states recognizes this, and is a male version of survival—two physical and emotional equals duking it out or facing off *High Noon* style, pistols at the ready. Burning beds, parents united in abuse in their family den—these are not the images our male legislators had in mind when the criminal codes were written.

We've learned a lot since then about the psychology of abusive relationships, about the cruelty, oppression and inescapability of child abuse and molestation, about the terror that marks virtually every moment for the victims of chronic domestic violence. Despite this knowledge, the media, the self-anointed pundits and the self-promoting denizens of the law schools' ivory towers sanctimoniously declare their outrage when an abused person recounts a life of torment to explain why he or she succumbed at last to terror and struck out at the abuser. These critics label such explanations the "abuse excuse." They lament our loss of "personal responsibility."

The Battered Women's Syndrome Defense Rectifies Bias

Charles P. Ewing, professor of law at the State University of New York at Buffalo, and others feel that the growth in acceptance of the battered women's syndrome doesn't reflect a loosening of standards so much as an attempt to rectify gender bias in the legal system and incorporate medical knowledge into the law.

Historically, raising self-defense claims for battered women has been "like fitting a square peg into a round hole," says Ewing. There were problems in proving they acted reasonably by staying in an abusive situation and by resorting to violence when there appeared to be no imminent threat of danger. What was not grasped, says Richard A. Rosen of the University of North Carolina's law clinic, is that "a battered woman is always in danger. It's like being kidnapped. Even when you're asleep you're at risk."

Legally, the only option for these women was to claim insanity in homicide cases. But that strategy changed as juries became educated about "learned helplessness"—in part by TV talk shows and movies of the week. Juries came to understand why victims would feel as if they had no options other than lethal force.

Stephanie B. Goldberg, *ABA Journal*, June 1994.

This male model of justice pervades the public consciousness and explains why many people say they would sympathize with O.J. Simpson even if they believe he killed Nicole Brown Simpson and Ronald Goldman. It wouldn't matter, they say, even if they believed that these killings followed years in which this strong, physically fit professional athlete beat and emotionally abused his five-foot-eight 125-pound wife. O.J. Simpson may indeed be innocent, as he is now legally presumed to be. What makes much of his support in the community troubling, however, is that it derives not from this presumption, but from the undercurrent of entitlement that the killing of an ex-wife engenders.

A Case of Psychological Abuse

The best and worst example of this double standard was graphically displayed to me in a case I handled a decade ago. My client, then a woman of fifty, had been raped on her way home from work years before and traumatized by the experience. Twenty years later she married a widower with a four-year-old daughter—and a shadowy past. Only after marrying this wealthy, domineering man did my client discover that he had produced his widowerhood by shooting his unarmed first wife to death as she spoke to a friend on the telephone while his infant daughter slept in the next room. He was convicted of manslaughter, served less than two years in prison and regained custody of the little girl upon his release.

During the course of their ten-year marriage the husband's highest form of amusement was to play the role of my client's former rapist by sneaking up on her from behind and grabbing her. He was the textbook battering husband, jealous, possessive, controlling his wife's every movement and human contact, belittling, explosively angry, sexually demanding. Finally, after a period of especially frequent outbursts, he threatened to do to my client what he had done to his first wife. She shot him, once, in the head while he was sleeping. She ran screaming down the hallway, called the police, confessed her crime. At her first trial she was convicted of second-degree murder and sentenced to five years to life in state prison. Her conviction was reversed on appeal due to prosecutorial and judicial misconduct.

That's when I entered the case. In her second trial, we presented evidence of the extreme psychological impairment this woman suffered. The jury hung; subsequently, she pleaded guilty to manslaughter and the judge granted her probation. At the sentencing hearing, the male deputy D.A. took my client's hand and said: "I want to apologize to you for that first conviction. You are not a murderer. I just didn't understand."

Score one for equal justice.

"Although a woman who kills an abusive husband may seem more sympathetic than a man who kills an unfaithful wife, there are striking parallels."

Battered Woman Syndrome Should Not Be a Legal Defense

Stanton Peele

Battered woman syndrome has been used as a legal defense by women who have killed their spouses. In the following viewpoint, Stanton Peele compares the battered woman defense to the betrayed man defense, where a husband kills his unfaithful wife in a jealous rage. He argues that if feminists push for acceptance of the battered woman defense, they may end up justifying homicide by "betrayed men." Peele is a psychologist and the author of *Diseasing of America: How We Allowed Recovery Zealots and the Treatment Industry to Convince Us We Are Out of Control.*

As you read, consider the following questions:

1. According to Judith A. Wolfer, cited by the author, why should judges treat the murder of a spouse the same as any other homicide?
2. What alternative to murder do battered women and betrayed men have, according to Peele?
3. What does Stephen Schulhofer, cited by the author, say juries tend to think in cases where men kill unfaithful wives?

What do you call it when a woman kills her spouse? If the husband had a history of abusing and intimidating her, the homicide may be considered an expression of "battered-woman syndrome." Because of repeated abuse, the theory goes, the battered woman has low self-esteem. Depressed and unmotivated, she is unable to leave her husband. She comes to believe that the only way of extricating herself is to maim or kill him. Even though she is not in immediate danger at the time she strikes back (if she were, she could plead self-defense), promoters of battered-woman syndrome argue that she should be treated leniently.

Battered Women vs. Betrayed Men

Now what do you call it when a man kills *his* spouse? For Kenneth Peacock, a trucker in Towson, Maryland, the answer was "manslaughter." Mr. Peacock, who shot his wife in the head after he came home at night to find her in bed with another man, received an eighteen-month sentence on October 17, 1994. Judge Robert E. Cahill sympathized with the perpetrator. "I seriously wonder how many men married five, four years would have the strength to walk away without inflicting some corporal punishment," he remarked. Judge Cahill couldn't think of a situation that would provoke "an uncontrollable rage greater than this: for someone who is happily married to be betrayed in your personal life, when you're out working to support the spouse." The judge almost apologized for sentencing Mr. Peacock: "I am forced to impose a sentence . . . only because I think I must do it to make the system honest."

Law students at the University of Maryland immediately organized protests. Patricia Ireland, director of the National Organization for Women, promised a national campaign to make sentences tougher for men who kill their wives. "This judge is excusing this behavior by giving this lenient sentence," said Maryland attorney Judith A. Wolfer. "Until judges start treating a homicide of a spouse as any other homicide, men are going to continue to kill their wives with impunity for reasons of jealousy, control, or rage. You name it, they'll use it."

Double Standards

Ironically, Miss Wolfer has been a prominent advocate of the battered-woman defense, which hardly "treat[s] homicide of a spouse as any other homicide." In 1991 she and the group she represents, the House of Ruth, successfully lobbied Maryland governor William Schaefer to pardon eight women who were serving long sentences for assaulting or killing their husbands (following a similar move by Ohio governor Richard F. Celeste in December 1990). She and her colleagues presented the governor with dossiers that described abuse allegedly committed by the women's husbands.

Although a woman who kills an abusive husband may seem more sympathetic than a man who kills an unfaithful wife, there are striking parallels between the leniency Miss Wolfer condemns and the leniency she advocates. Both hinge on a spouse's misbehavior and its impact on the defendant's state of mind. Neither is based on an argument of self-defense. Indeed, the homicide often does not immediately follow the provocation. Mr. Peacock shot his wife four hours after chasing away her lover; in the interim, he drank and argued with her. Francine Hughes, whose story inspired the film *The Burning Bed*, set her husband on fire as he slept.

Battered Women Are Not Insane

The battered woman syndrome theory holds that due to repeated battering, "the victim becomes completely passive," says Cathy Young, vice president of the Women's Freedom Network. "It's an interesting sort of reasoning because it assumes the woman is so passive she can't leave a relationship, but she's not too passive to kill."

So battered woman syndrome equals insanity, right? Wrong. Insanity long has been recognized as a defense by courts. . . . "Basically, it seems like a grab bag of justifications that can be used to justify just about anything," says Young.

Michael Fumento, *Insight*, February 6, 1995.

Both the battered woman and the betrayed man have an alternative: they can leave. (Mrs. Hughes, like many battered women, had separated from her husband several times, only to return to him voluntarily.) When the wronged spouse does not simply leave, we are told, it is because he or she has been incapacitated by the circumstances; the battered-woman defense emphasizes the female stereotype of passivity, while the betrayed-man defense emphasizes the male stereotype of jealous rage. Given these similarities, it's not surprising that the attorney who got Mr. Peacock such a light sentence, David B. Irwin, has been equally successful in representing women who killed their husbands.

One-Time Killers?

Critics of both the Maryland and the Ohio pardons argued that the governors heard only information favorable to the prisoners and did not examine the trial transcripts. The *Baltimore Sun* noted that one of the women released in Maryland had hired a hit man and collected on her dead husband's insurance policy. Governor Schaefer responded by describing the emotional testimony of the prisoners he had interviewed, most of whom were not likely to commit additional crimes. But jailed assailants often seem contrite. Judge Cahill had the same impression of Mr. Peacock: "I have no question in my mind that no judge . . . will ever see Kenneth Peacock again," he said. Mr. Peacock had no criminal record, and the prosecutor noted that *Mrs.* Peacock's mother sympathized with her son-in-law.

Maryland attorney general J. Joseph Curran Jr. criticized the prosecutor, Assistant State's Attorney Michael G. DeHaven, for agreeing to the manslaughter plea. Mr. Curran rejected the notion that men who have found their wives *in flagrante delicto* are justified in killing them. The appropriate response, he said, is divorce. Of course, the same could be said for battered women, but Mr. Curran did not publicly object to Governor Schaefer's pardons in 1991.

Curran argued that Peacock's sentence was based on retrograde thinking. Yet manslaughter pleas are still typical in cases like this one. Stephen Schulhofer, a criminologist at the University of Chicago, says juries "tend to think it is reasonable for men to lose it when they hear about adultery." Modern courts have consistently accepted a wife's adultery as a mitigating factor in homicide cases.

Critics of this practice note that it may invite husbands who kill in cold blood to claim that they lost their heads after learning of their wives' infidelity. The battered-woman defense poses a similar danger. In some cases the women have indeed suffered a long history of egregious abuse. In 1985, for example, New Jersey governor Tom Kean pardoned Joyce Bunch, who had been sentenced to seven years in prison for the non-fatal shooting of her husband. Over the years her husband's attacks had left her unconscious, disfigured, and in one instance temporarily paralyzed. But Mrs. Bunch's case does not appear to be typical. The *Columbus Dispatch* reported that fifteen of the twenty-five women pardoned by Governor Celeste in 1990 said they had not been physically abused. Six had discussed killing their husbands beforehand, and two had tracked down men from whom they were separated.

Since men are much more likely to kill women than vice versa, feminists should hesitate before broadening the excuses available to murderers. It is tempting to say that a man's outrageous conduct justifies lenient treatment of his wife when she kills him. But the Peacock case shows that such logic cuts both ways.

"If the battered woman syndrome is a kind of excuse, it's a far better excuse, and far more deserving of being heard."

Battered Woman Syndrome Should Be a Legal Defense

Glamour

Battered woman syndrome is one of many abuse syndromes that have been used as a legal defense. In the following viewpoint, the editors of *Glamour* magazine argue that unlike other "abuse excuses," battered woman syndrome is often a valid criminal defense. In order for judges and juries to fairly respond to an abused woman's circumstances, the terror and powerlessness she experiences must be properly explained to them, according to the editors. *Glamour* is a monthly fashion magazine.

As you read, consider the following questions:

1. What is the worst aspect of the spread of "victimism" and "designer defenses," in the authors' opinion?
2. According to the authors, what are some examples of defendants who have traditionally been allowed to make excuses?
3. In the authors' opinion, who can and should distinguish between real victims and excusemongers?

Editorial, "Not Guilty on Grounds of Being a Victim," *Glamour*, July 1994, p. 68. Reprinted by permission of the author, Tessa Decarlo.

It's one of the achievements of the late twentieth century that the widespread trauma of abuse is finally being recognized and its effects on behavior understood. Yet there's a dark side. Claiming "I'm a victim too" seems to be an increasingly popular way to duck responsibility for everything from poor job performance to murder.

A data processor in Philadelphia sued to get his job back after he was fired for being late to work every day. He claimed that his upbringing in a dysfunctional family had disabled him by creating a "neurotic compulsion for lateness."

The Popularity of Designer Defenses

When an eighteen-year-old Milwaukee, Wisconsin, girl shot and killed another teenager to get a leather coat, she pleaded not guilty by reason of insanity. Her attorney argued that the killing was not intentional because her client suffered from "urban psychosis," a variant of post-traumatic stress disorder in which the stresses of inner-city life, compounded by child abuse, create borderline personality disorder.

A young nanny in Westchester County, New York, was convicted of killing her ten-month-old charge by hurling him to the floor. Prior to sentencing, her lawyer asked for leniency because the marijuana the nanny had smoked a few hours before the incident had triggered "adult attention-deficit disorder."

The popularity of such "designer defenses" increases every time they are used successfully for high-profile defendants like Lyle and Erik Menendez [whose trial for murder of their parents resulted in hung juries in January 1994]. "The word gets around that this is the way to beat the rap," says William C. O'Malley, president of the National District Attorneys Association. "I can assure you that right now someone is watching TV or reading a popular magazine and thinking, 'Maybe this will work for me.' "

Even celebrity defense attorney Alan Dershowitz, who successfully appealed Claus von Bulow's attempted-murder conviction, thinks the pendulum has swung too far. "The message that [the Menendez case] sends to abused or allegedly abused people," he said recently on national television, is "that if you can come up with an abuse excuse, you can literally get away with murder."

"Victimism" makes for bad criminal justice and bad social policy. Perhaps worst of all, the backlash against the excesses of "the abuse excuse" now threatens those who really are victims, particularly victims of domestic violence.

Battered Woman Syndrome

In recent years, battered woman syndrome has become a sometimes-successful defense for women who, having suffered years of brutal physical abuse, and having been failed by their families, the police and the courts, finally kill their abuser to save their own and sometimes their children's lives. Is there a difference between abuse excuses and these women's claim that victimhood justified their violence?

According to traditional readings of the law, no. By that standard, a history of abuse and the woman's perception of her own danger are irrelevant in court. All that matters is: Did she kill him or not? As Dershowitz put it in his TV discussion of the abuse excuse, "Why should [battered women] be able to tell the jury they were abused, if the vast majority of people who are abused don't kill?" When the game is played by those rules, these women are usually punished severely—often far more severely than male batterers who kill their female victims.

Battered Women's Syndrome in the Courts

Even if, as many seem to think, the average juror is growing more receptive to the idea that criminal impulses are sometimes excusable, there is nothing to suggest that courts share this enthusiasm. And they, after all, are the gatekeepers who decide whether this evidence gets in or not.

Consider:

While testimony about battered women's syndrome is admissible in just about every state, it came as the result of a hard-fought, fifteen-year-long struggle, say advocates. And the battle continues. In some states, the requirement of proof of imminent danger still prevents some battered women from claiming self-defense, says Richard A. Rosen, a law professor at the University of North Carolina in Chapel Hill.

Stephanie B. Goldberg, *ABA Journal*, June 1994.

Once defense lawyers were permitted to explain these women's terror, isolation and powerlessness as battered woman syndrome, says Sheila Kuehl, counsel to the California Women's Law Center, prosecutors, judges and juries were able to see battered women's circumstances more clearly and deal with them more fairly.

"Some may think all these women are just whining," adds Kuehl. "But [the success of the battered woman defense] is happening because we're finally letting the truths about abuse and what it does to people's lives into the courtroom."

When we resist victim excuses, we're resisting an abdication of personal responsibility. But outrage over the more preposterous victimism defenses shouldn't keep us from admitting that our legal system has always allowed some defendants to make excuses. How often have kids from "good families" gotten a slap on the wrist for crimes that earned jail time for youngsters with less skillful attorneys and darker skins? How many thousands of men have gotten away with murder because the women they killed "provoked" them, or because they were drunk, or because they acted in the heat of passion? If the battered woman syndrome is a kind of excuse, it's a far better excuse, and far more deserving of being heard.

This excuse, like any other, can be falsely invoked. But deciding who has a case and who doesn't is the jury's job. "Limiting the kinds of defenses that people are allowed to use means limiting what information juries are allowed to know," says Kim Gandy, the National Organization for Women's executive vice president. "If you give the jury all the facts, I believe they're capable of making the right decision."

A Distinction Can Be Made

And so far, judges and juries have been far more likely to turn down abuse excuses than to buy them. The chronic-lateness argument was thrown out of court, and both the Milwaukee shooter and the Westchester nanny were sentenced to heavy jail time. Even in the Menendez case, in which an abuse excuse was particularly well received, the jurors were divided over whether the brothers should be convicted of murder or manslaughter—not over acquittal.

In most cases, it's clearly possible to tell the real victims from the excusemongers. "It's patently absurd to compare a woman who defends herself against a long-term abusive partner with some person who says he robbed a liquor store because he grew up eating too many Twinkies," says Michael Dowd, director of the Battered Women's Justice Center at New York's Pace University. "If we as a society can't make that distinction, it's not because there's something wrong with battered woman syndrome. It's because there's something wrong with us."

===

"Crime victims should have a voice."

===

The Justice System Should Consider the Rights of Victims

Roberta Roper, interviewed by *American Legion Magazine*

An increasing number of states are allowing victims of crime to introduce statements about the crime's impact on them as a consideration in the sentencing of defendants. In the following viewpoint, Roberta Roper argues in favor of a role for victims at criminal trials, rejecting claims by defense lawyers and others that victims' participation tips the scales of justice and biases juries. Roper is the founder of the Stephanie Roper Committee and Foundation, a victims' rights advocacy group. *American Legion* magazine is published monthly by the American Legion, a military-service veterans organization.

As you read, consider the following questions:

1. What three things do victims and survivors want from the criminal justice system, according to Roper?
2. Why does Roper say she was not allowed to testify at the trial of her daughter's killer?

Excerpted from "When Justice Robs the Victims of Crime," an interview with Roberta Roper, *American Legion Magazine*, February 1995. Reprinted with permission.

In 1982, Stephanie Roper was a twenty-two-year-old college senior who had gone out for a few drinks with friends in Washington, D.C. On her way home, she ran out of gas alone on a Maryland country road. Two men stopped to help her.

The "good samaritans" kidnapped, raped, tortured and murdered her. They were planning to dismember her body when someone tipped off the police. Both men confessed to the crime. One pleaded guilty; the other went to trial. . . .

Roberta Roper, Stephanie's mother, is credited with almost single-handedly pushing nearly three dozen laws through the Maryland legislature. These measures provide restitution to crime victims, give victims the right to file impact statements with the courts, and order courts to notify victims of all hearings involving their assailants. The Stephanie Roper Committee and Foundation has become one of the largest victims' rights organizations in the country. . . .

The Victims' Rights Agenda

American Legion: *Just what do victims and survivors want from the justice system?*

Roberta Roper: First, victims and survivors want the system to give them information, even if it's painful information. You can deal with the terrible truth. What you can't deal with is not knowing.

Second, you want a certain amount of compassion and understanding. Third, you want satisfaction with the process—that your loved one who is a homicide victim is not just another statistic, a faceless stranger.

The measure of an effective system is how it treats people and whether victims are allowed some choices. Not every victim wants to be in the courtroom. Not every victim wants restitution. Not every victim wants to make a victim-impact statement. But the choices should be there.

I'm not suggesting that the victim's interest be represented by an attorney, that there be a three-party system. But the state of Maryland didn't bleed and die; Stephanie did. We want justice—not revenge.

What about stiffer sentences?

You can talk to a roomful of victims and they'll be far more reasonable and moderate than the average citizen who says, "Lock them up and throw away the key!" Victims quickly learn how the system works and most don't have a clear expectation about a specific sentence. We want appropriate punishment.

Our horror was that life meant so little. In Stephanie's case, it seemed like a misuse of language that her killers got two life sentences plus twenty years, and they would be eligible for parole in eleven and a half years.

What about the claim that protecting victims' rights gives an unfair advantage to middle-class victims?

When we started, one legislator said that we were anti-black, pro–death penalty and had blood dripping from our hands. Others say victim-impact statements are unfair because some victims, homeless people, for example, would have nobody to speak for them.

To say that survivors or victims should not be allowed to speak because one might be more articulate than another is to subject us to an unfair standard. Look at the other players in the system. Some of the prosecutors or the attorneys are not very competent or articulate. Besides, a victim-impact statement is just another piece of information that the court can accept or reject.

Victims Should Be Heard

The victims' rights movement continues to gain momentum. On Election Day in 1992, voters in Illinois, Missouri, Kansas, Colorado, and New Mexico approved amendments to their constitutions that accord victims of crimes the right to be both present and heard during court proceedings.

This guarantee seems almost incidental. Many of us assume that the interests of victims are adequately represented in criminal trials. But nothing could be further from the truth. America's criminal justice system is tilted decidedly in favor of the criminal as opposed to the victim.

Joseph Perkins, *Washington Times*, November 12, 1992.

You have fought for the right of victims or their survivors to be heard at assailants' trials. Defense lawyers say this tips the scales of justice.

I believe that crime victims should have a voice—not a veto, not a mandate—but a voice.

At the trial of one of Stephanie's killers, the defense succeeded in preventing the jury from seeing a photograph of her body on the grounds that it was inflammatory. I was not allowed to testify on the grounds that whatever I said would be emotional, irrelevant and probable cause for a mistrial.

However, we heard the killer plead for his life in court. We heard his father and his wife. We heard a jailhouse minister say Stephanie's murderer had found God and was extremely remorseful.

A former friend from the fire department was allowed to testify. So was his child's teacher.

You sound so reasonable. Why do you think you were so vilified when you started your campaign?

I don't know. People made judgments about us. A columnist in the *Washington Post* wrote, "Stephanie Roper had once been a beautiful baby, a lovely young woman. Now she was the name of an ill-begotten cause and her parents either had a knack for public relations or were being exploited by others."

I called the columnist and asked if he was a parent and what he would have done if Stephanie had been his child. He answered as people typically do, "If it had been my kid, I would have shot the SOB." Yet he thought the system had acted properly.

Now the pendulum has swung. There is widespread sentiment for victims' rights and an Office for Victims of Crime in the Department of Justice. What made the difference?

Sheer numbers. Read the papers, turn on the TV. In the past many people thought that crime was something that happens to other people—that victims did things to somehow place their lives at risk. Now one in four families experiences violent crime. Random violence is happening to people we know and love. Crime is no longer someone else's problem.

But credit for changing the justice system is also due to grassroots efforts of victims and survivors. We have been the catalysts in that process. We have reminded the legislators and the public that the system doesn't belong to judges, prosecutors and lawyers. The justice system is supposed to do the people's business.

"Will some vengeful victims, by injecting their wishes formally into the process, tip the scales so that the influence and standing of the victims drives the severity of the sentences?"

The Justice System Should Not Overemphasize the Rights of Victims

Andrew L. Sonner

Victims' rights laws, including the right to make victim impact statements at criminal trials, have been enacted by a few states. In the following viewpoint, Andrew L. Sonner argues that caution should be exercised when such legislation is enacted. Victim impact statements may result in unequal sentences for criminals guilty of similar crimes, Sonner contends, and victims' rights reforms may cause trials to be delayed, which will make victims less happy with the process. Sonner is the state attorney for Montgomery County, Maryland.

As you read, consider the following questions:

1. Why is the criminal justice system currently being attacked by some observers, according to Sonner?
2. What are the problems created by consulting with victims at every significant stage of the process, in the author's opinion?

Originally published in the July 22, 1994, *CQ Researcher*, as Andrew L. Sonner's views on the At Issue section's topic, "Are New Laws Needed to Protect Crime Victims' Rights?" Reprinted by permission of Congressional Quarterly, Inc.

In some jurisdictions, prosecutors, police and judges—not to mention defense attorneys—treat victims callously. A civilized justice system should not do that. It should ease the burdens of victims.

But legislative efforts designed to improve the treatment of victims should be subjected to rigorous scrutiny to assure that the collateral consequences of well-intentioned reforms do not damage public prosecution or fundamental fairness. Several states are finding that they have built in expensive delays and additional work without improving victim satisfaction. The solution should be no broader than the problem.

Some Questions Should Be Addressed

Victims' rights legislation first poses a fundamental philosophical question: How much should the personal feelings of victims influence the outcome of criminal cases? One of the goals of justice is the impartial administration of sanctions so that equally culpable defendants do not receive disparate punishment. American criminal justice is currently under attack by some informed observers for what is perceived as unfairly prosecuting and sentencing minorities. Will some vengeful victims, by injecting their wishes formally into the process, tip the scales so that the influence and standing of the victims drives the severity of the sentences?

Victim Impact Statements and Equal Sentences

Under the current state of the law, the victim has the greatest power at the stage where he or she least deserves and needs it—at sentencing. As a structural matter, the system can tolerate victim input at the time of sentencing, for at that stage everything is admissible. Everyone in town has a say about what should be done with a convicted felon. The victim too might as well fuel the public's lust for vengeance or promote the virtue of forgiveness. It would be a mistake, however, to privilege this input from the victim and treat it as critical to a proper level of punishment.

Punishment responds to the wrong the offender commits, but not to the particular wrong as measured by victims willing to testify. Killing a homeless beggar is as great a wrong as depriving a family of a loved one. Or at least that is what we have always assumed about homicide. It hardly makes sense to think of life as sacred if its value is a function of how much others love or need the person killed. That the victim is a human being is sufficient to determine the evil of killing.

George P. Fletcher, *With Justice for Some: Victims' Rights in Criminal Trials*, 1995.

159

There are also practical questions for legislators to consider in victims' rights legislation. To whom should the legislation apply? Making the rights apply to all victims of crime not only entails enormous costs, but often involuntarily injects victims more deeply into prosecution than is warranted or than many of them want. . . .

Some proposed legislation requires that law enforcement and the court "consult" with victims at every "significant stage." Does that include the charging stage, preliminary hearing, grand jury, plea negotiations, sentencing and appeal? And what will be the remedy for violations of victims' rights? How will those remedies be enforced? May victims address the court to express disagreement with prosecutors' charges, plea agreements or sentencing recommendations?

At the state level, the victims' rights movement's strategy has been to marshal crime victims with brutal experiences to recount their insensitive treatment by an impersonal system. Their stories can lead officials to legislate by anecdote. . . .

Some proposed reforms are tempting opportunities for a symbolic "going on the record for victims," but are poorly tailored to address defects in treatment. Ill-considered reforms themselves may quickly need reforming. Every citizen deserves understanding and courteous treatment from government officials, but a proper regard for justice calls for caution when trying to achieve it by legislation.

"Punitive damages have replaced baseball as our national sport."

Liability Lawsuits Hurt Consumers

Theodore B. Olson

Many attorneys and legislators have decried the litigiousness of Americans and have called for reform of jury awards to victims in civil suits. In the following viewpoint, Theodore B. Olson argues that excessive punitive damage awards, such as the one in the *Exxon Valdez* oil spill case, do not prompt businesses to improve the safety of their products or operations; they simply impose hidden costs on investors and consumers. Olson is an attorney in Washington, D.C., and a former assistant attorney general in the U.S. Justice Department.

As you read, consider the following questions:

1. According to Olson, who will pay the $5 billion punitive fine imposed on Exxon?
2. In what way is the civil justice system like a lottery and in what way is it like bullfighting, in Olson's opinion?
3. What does the author say is the real cost of excessive jury awards?

An Alaska jury in September 1994 imposed the largest punitive fine in the history of the world on the shareholders of Exxon Corporation. The $5 billion punitive damage award will be shared by 34,000 of the jurors' fellow Alaskans—about $150,000 per plaintiff before deductions for attorneys' fees.

The verdict, unless reduced, will be five times greater than the largest previous civil punishment ever. And it dwarfs the maximum criminal fine that could be imposed under federal or state law for even the most calculated, heinous and brutal offense.

An Outrageous Award

Not a penny of the award will go toward cleaning up Prince William Sound or compensating those who were injured as a result of the 1989 *Exxon Valdez* oil spill. Exxon has already spent $2.5 billion to clean up the damage, and the jury previously awarded another $300 million to compensate fully the fishermen and others who were injured by the spill. In addition, in 1991 Exxon agreed to pay nearly $1 billion to Alaska and the United States in fines and compensatory damages.

The cleanup was remarkably successful. While not every vestige of the spill has been expunged, most of it has. And the 1994 salmon run was the third most bountiful in history.

Thus, the $5 billion punishment serves no compensatory or restorative function. It is a pure windfall to those who were unfortunate enough to have been affected by the spill—now fully compensated for their injuries—but also fortunate enough to be the latest beneficiaries of America's capricious and whimsical punitive damage system.

Besides providing the equivalent of a jackpot for 34,000 Alaskans and their attorneys (who will undoubtedly be the biggest winners by far), the $5 billion punitive damage award serves no constructive societal function and is actually quite harmful and counterproductive.

Punitive damages are supposed to punish and deter. But this regrettable incident has already cost Exxon more than $3.5 billion dollars in fines, damages and cleanup costs. The accident was allegedly caused by a second mate who failed to execute a proper command and by a captain's failure to remain on the ship's bridge. If mistakes and human errors such as these can ever be completely prevented, Exxon's $3.5 billion price tag so far is more than adequate incentive to Exxon or any other company to see that everything is done to ensure that it will never happen again.

In any event, the $5 billion in punitive damages is completely misdirected punishment. No ship captain, tanker officer or Exxon official will pay this judgment. It will be taken entirely from Exxon stockholders, many of whom are pension trusts, endowments and retirees, who did nothing wrong and warrant no punishment or deterrence. There is no rational basis for extracting $500 from every one of Exxon's roughly 1,000,000 stockholders and giving it to 34,000 fully compensated Alaskans and their attorneys.

Reprinted by permission: Tribune Media Services.

The Exxon punitive damage award is just the latest and most egregious manifestation of a civil justice system that is running amok. In New Mexico in August 1994, a jury returned a $2.7 million punitive damage verdict against McDonald's because a woman in a car spilled very hot coffee on herself. In September 1994, a San Francisco jury assessed a $6.9 million fine against a law firm for "failing to do more" to discipline a former partner in a sexual harassment case. In October 1991, a Chicago jury slapped a pharmaceutical company for $125 million because its product was misadministered by a doctor resulting in the loss of an eye. In Texas in 1992, a wrongful employee termination resulted in an $80 million punitive damage verdict. Alabama attorneys regularly give campaign contributions to judges before whom they try cases. Juries there awarded them more than $200 million in punitive damages in 1994 alone, mostly against out-of-state insurance companies and financial institutions.

A $500,000 punitive damage award used to be a rarity; now

such verdicts are commonplace. The Alaska Exxon verdict is the equal of 10,000 such awards.

Punitive damages have replaced baseball as our national sport. The system is a perverse combination of lottery and bullfighting, selecting beneficiaries and targets almost at random and inflicting brutal punishment on the latter if they wander into the arena; in the case of punitive damages, of course, the arena is a courtroom. The game is won by those who can claim some injury—however remote or speculative—at the hands of a wealthy and distant corporation and who can persuade a jury to "send a message" to Wilmington, Delaware, or Hartford, Connecticut, or wherever corporate headquarters may be. As the U.S. Supreme Court said in 1994, juries "use their verdicts to express their biases against big businesses, particularly those without strong local presences."

The punitive damage losers are not the corporations but the stockholders who must pay the judgments from the treasuries that their investments created. The ultimate victims, of course, are policyholders and consumers who pay these judgments through higher prices, narrower product choices and tepid coffee. Often taxpayers wind up paying punitive damages that are increasingly assessed against cities and counties.

The Hidden Costs

Although some excessive jury verdicts are reduced by judges, many are not, and the real cost is the hidden one in the thousands of cases that are settled for otherwise unrealistic amounts because of the threat of crippling punitive damages. This underwater portion of the iceberg, along with the verdicts actually paid, is passed along to the consumer in the form of, for example, more expensive ladders and private aircraft, and in such intangible costs as excessive testing by doctors and warning labels on everything from vitamin pills to hotel suites.

The final irony is that punitive damages produce a Gresham's law of corporate responsibility. If Exxon is to be whacked $5 billion despite its unprecedented and massive effort to restore Prince William Sound, tomorrow's corporations may see little incentive in reacting responsibly to accidents. Or they may avoid dangerous and high-risk ventures altogether and sell their tankers to Liberian or Panamanian companies that may be difficult to sue or unable to pay for their misadventures. Responsible entrepreneurs will be replaced over time by irresponsible ones. In the end, the public will pay dearly for our irrational and punitive civil justice system.

"*The tort system is one place where the average citizen can battle the powerful on nearly equal terms.*"

Liability Lawsuits Help Consumers

Carl T. Bogus

Legislation proposed in Congress in 1995 sought to reform the civil tort system by capping jury awards to victims and discouraging frivolous lawsuits. In the following viewpoint, Carl T. Bogus opposes such legislative efforts, arguing that lawsuits and large punitive damage awards have been successful in prompting businesses to take dangerous products off the market, thus improving public safety. Bogus is a visiting professor at Rutgers University School of Law in Camden, New Jersey.

As you read, consider the following questions:

1. According to Bogus, what has the products liability system accomplished time and again?
2. What does the author say is a common occurrence with jury verdicts involving large settlements?
3. What percentage of retail product sales accounts for added insurance costs, according to figures cited by Bogus?

The tort system, and products liability in particular, is a bone stuck in the throat of big business. The tort system is one place where the average citizen can battle the powerful on nearly equal terms. The contingent fee arrangement, in which the attorney's fee comes from the recovery in the case, makes it possible for someone who has been seriously injured by an unreasonably dangerous product to retain the kind of top legal talent that most people otherwise could never afford. Moreover, in the litigation discovery process, business must allow the plaintiff's attorneys to examine its files and question its research scientists, engineers, and managers. This process often forces the darkest corporate secrets—including those previously concealed from government regulators—into the floodlight of a public courtroom.

An Unreasonably Dangerous Car

One of the earliest and most famous products liability cases illustrates how this works. In 1969 Ford Motor Company made a deliberate decision to produce a new subcompact, the Pinto, with a gas tank that its executives knew was prone to explode in minor collisions. Lee Iacocca, then executive vice president of Ford [now chairman of General Motors], had decreed that the Pinto must sell for no more than $2,000 and weigh no more than 2,000 pounds; these requirements forced Ford to depart from usual engineering practices. Crash tests on prototypes revealed that when the Pinto was rear-ended at speeds as low as 21 miles per hour, the fuel tank ruptured and gasoline sometimes flooded the driver's compartment. Ford engineers proposed a variety of ways to fix the problem. However, even relatively minor and inexpensive modifications threatened Iacocca's cost and weight decree, and management vetoed them all. . . .

A jury in a products liability case awarded Richard Grimshaw, a thirteen-year-old boy who would spend twenty years undergoing surgeries and skin grafts for burns he received when his aunt's Pinto exploded, $2.5 million in compensatory damages and $125 million in punitive damages (later reduced to $3.5 million by the court). In discovery, Grimshaw's lawyers had learned about the crash tests and Ford's decision not to correct the problem. Shortly thereafter, the National Highway Traffic Safety Administration (NHTSA) initiated action to compel Ford to recall the 1.5 million Pintos on the road.

The Ford Pinto is merely one of many such stories. The products liability system has repeatedly exposed grave risks to public safety and driven dangerous products from the market. Time and again, it has unearthed secret files showing that companies knew about product hazards but concealed that information from regulators and the public. This was the case with asbestos,

166

the Dalkon Shield [contraceptive IUD], and General Motors pickup trucks (a case that bears an eerie similarity to the Pinto story). George L. Priest, a conservative Yale Law School professor, remarked: "No one conscious of the dwindling budget and meager accomplishments of the Consumer Product Safety Commission can pretend that the United States makes a serious effort to regulate product quality directly. Instead, our society relies on liability actions to police the manufacturing process.". . .

Tales of the Absurd

Republicans may not have included tort reform in the 1994–1995 Contract with America [a campaign platform and legislative agenda adopted by Republican members of the House of Representatives] out of popular demand, yet in recent years Republican politicians have succeeded in making it a reasonably popular issue. They have done so by ridiculing government, in this case by portraying the judicial system as an Alice in Wonderland world of greedy lawyers and Mad Hatter judges. In a speech on the Senate floor on July 27, 1994, for example, Senator John Danforth told a story about a case involving a seventy-year-old man who lost sight in one eye. "This person filed a lawsuit, a products liability case, against the Upjohn Company, and his recovery was $127 million," Danforth told his colleagues.

This was a gross distortion. A jury had rendered a verdict of $127 million against Upjohn, but not because it deemed that to be "reasonable compensation" for the plaintiff's loss. More than $124 million of the award was punitive damages, to punish Upjohn for promoting its drug, Depo-Medrol, for use in a manner that was not approved by the Food and Drug Administration and without warning physicians about the risks. Indeed, Upjohn had so effectively marketed its drug for this unapproved purpose (injecting it near the eye) that ophthalmologists were using it this way one million times per year. As is common with jury verdicts involving large settlements, the courts reduced the award. The plaintiff's final recovery, including both compensatory and punitive damages, was about $6 million.

Dan Quayle told audiences about a psychic who won a jury award of nearly $1 million because a CAT scan allegedly robbed her of her psychic powers, but he neglected to mention that the judge dismissed the award. Ronald Reagan recounted how a cat burglar sued a homeowner for injuries incurred while falling through the homeowner's skylight. When the real case was identified, it turned out that the plaintiff was not a cat burglar at all. He was a high school student who had been sent to retrieve athletic equipment stored on the roof of the school and had fallen through a skylight that had been painted black.

We will almost certainly hear more about the August 1994

case of the woman who won a $2.9 million jury verdict against McDonald's after burning herself with a cup of hot coffee. But don't expect to hear that McDonald's coffee is heated between 180 and 190 degrees Fahrenheit, while coffee made at home is between 130 and 140 degrees; that over the past ten years McDonald's received 700 reports of patrons burning themselves with its superheated coffee; or that the eighty-one-year-old plaintiff was hospitalized for eight days and underwent skin graft operations for third-degree burns. Don't expect to hear, as well, that the court reduced the $2.9 million jury verdict for punitive damages to $480,000, or that the jury found that the plaintiff was 20 percent responsible for her injuries (presumably because her injuries would have been only one-fifth as severe if the coffee had been 140 degrees) and that her compensatory award was reduced accordingly.

Reprinted by permission: Tribune Media Sevices.

We shall never know if a judge would have further reduced or even reversed the plaintiff's award on appeal because McDonald's elected to settle privately with the plaintiff. We do know, however, that following the McDonald's award, Wendy's voluntarily suspended selling hot chocolate—which it sold mostly to children and heated to a scalding 180 degrees—until it could lower the temperature. Reasonable people may disagree about whether there was merit to the McDonald's coffee case, but the system seems to serve the objective of prompting suppliers to make products safer.

The Mythical Flood

Yet even if the tales are mythical, is it true nevertheless that business is being strangled by liability suits in an "endless tide of litigation," as the Contract with America claims? Hardly. Contrary to the conventional wisdom, products liability litigation is not on the rise. The products liability caseload did increase substantially in the federal courts from 1975 to 1985. But from 1985 to 1990, products liability filings declined in the federal courts, and they have not increased since. In fact, plaintiffs' success rates and awards have been declining.

Second, products liability insurance costs vary widely depending on how potentially hazardous a particular product may be, but they generally are not as heavy a burden as business lobbyists suggest. A 1991 study by the National Insurance Consumer Organization found that the cost of insuring products liability, including both insurance premiums and the costs of self-insurance, constituted only 0.21 percent of retail product sales.

In surveys, businesses often say that they have withdrawn products from the market or decided not to market new products because of products liability; yet there is little hard data supporting such claims. Some bemoan the fact that liability is making diving boards harder to find at hotels and public pools, but when one considers that 1,000 people suffer spinal cord injuries in diving accidents each year, fewer diving boards may not be such a bad thing, particularly at shallow or unsupervised pools. The industry most often cited as an undeserving victim of products liability is general aviation (small planes). Although the U.S. general aviation industry lost its once dominant position in the world market, other factors were in play and it is not clear how much products liability was to blame. If products liability were driving desirable products from the market, business should have little trouble proving its case. Yet the evidence appears no stronger today than it was eighteen years ago when a federal interagency task force investigated similar claims and found that most products driven from the market were, in fact, unsafe.

Periodical Bibliography

The following articles have been selected to supplement the diverse views presented in this chapter. Addresses are provided for periodicals not indexed in the *Readers' Guide to Periodical Literature*, the *Alternative Press Index*, or the *Social Sciences Index*.

Jerry Adler	"Bloodied but Unbowed," *Newsweek*, April 3, 1995.
Mary Gaitskill	"On Not Being a Victim," *Harper's Magazine*, March 1994.
Mary Ann Glendon	"A Nation Under Lawyers," *American Enterprise*, November/December 1994. Available from 1150 17th St. NW, Washington, DC 20036.
Stephanie B. Goldberg	"Fault Lines," *ABA Journal*, June 1994. Available from 750 N. Lake Shore Dr., Chicago, IL 60611.
Sophfronia Scott Gregory	"Oprah! Oprah in the Court! Are Talk Shows Changing the Sensibilities of America's Jurors?" *Time*, June 6, 1994.
John Leo	"Watching 'As the Jury Turns,'" *U.S. News & World Report*, February 14, 1994.
John Leo	"The World's Most Litigious Nation," *U.S. News & World Report*, May 22, 1995.
National Review	"So Sue Them," April 3, 1995.
New Yorker	"Empty Suits," July 12, 1993.
Walter Olson	"Civil Suits," *Reason*, June 1995.
Virginia I. Postrel	"Lack of Conviction," *Reason*, March 1994.
Julia Reed	"Excuse Me," *Vogue*, May 1994.
Jeffrey Rosen	"Victim Justice," *New Republic*, April 17, 1995.
John Taylor	"Irresistible Impulses, Unbelievable Verdicts: Why America Has Lost Its Capacity to Convict the Guilty," *Esquire*, April 1994.
Hiller B. Zobel	"In Love with Lawsuits," *American Heritage*, November 1994.

For Further Discussion

Chapter 1

1. Martha T. McCluskey maintains that victimhood can give members of "victim" groups a voice of moral authority. In her opinion, how should this moral authority be used? According to Charles J. Sykes, what is the effect on society and on "victim" groups of the use of such moral authority?

2. Amitai Etzioni contends that a moral reawakening is necessary in American society. What evidence of moral decay does he present? What does he say communities can and should do to revitalize a sense of morality? Do Charles Edgley and Dennis Brissett argue that America is suffering from moral decay? Support your answer with examples from the viewpoints.

Chapter 2

1. Richard John Neuhaus argues that competition for entitlements among "victim" groups produces divisiveness in American culture. According to Neuhaus, what groups are responsible for this divisiveness? In Deval L. Patrick's opinion, what produces the divisiveness in American society? Support your answer using Patrick's viewpoint as evidence.

2. Amitai Etzioni calls for a moratorium on the creation of rights. In what ways would such a moratorium be harmful to American society, according to Samuel Walker?

3. Philip K. Howard notes many of the costs that businesses incur to comply with the Americans with Disabilities Act (ADA). List the examples he gives. Which do you find most persuasive, and why? According to David Wasserman, who should bear these costs? Do you agree with Wasserman that these are reasonable costs? Defend your answer with evidence from the viewpoints.

Chapter 3

1. Wendy Kaminer argues that self-help books overgeneralize the concept of codependence to apply to every problem that people face. What does Steve Hamilton say about the "one size fits all" quality of the family therapy approach? How do you think he would respond to Kaminer's argument? Explain your answer with evidence from the viewpoints.

2. Many advocates of repressed memory therapy contend that women who display certain symptoms of psychological problems may have suffered abuse even if they have no specific memory of it. According to Frederick Crews, what is the problem with this contention? In Ruth Wallen's opinion, what is the strength of the contention? Whose argument do you find more persuasive, and why?

3. Jill Nelson argues that rather than challenging stereotypes, talk shows exploit them for entertainment and profit. Does Joshua Gamson agree or disagree that talk shows exploit stereotypes for profit? Does he agree or disagree that talk shows challenge stereotypes? Which viewpoint do you agree with, and why?

Chapter 4

1. Defense lawyer Leslie Abramson describes a court case in which she defended a battered woman accused of murdering her husband. What was the outcome of that case, according to Abramson? What objections to this outcome do you think Alan Dershowitz would raise? What objections do you think author Stanton Peele would raise? Support your answer with evidence from the viewpoints.

2. Andrew L. Sonner argues that harsher sentences may be imposed in trials where a victim impact statement is introduced. What factors influence the harshness of sentences in such trials, according to Sonner? In Roberta Roper's opinion, what factors should influence the harshness of sentences?

3. Theodore B. Olson contends that the costs of punitive fines imposed in liability lawsuits are passed on to consumers. How does Carl T. Bogus respond to this argument? What example does Olson present to illustrate his argument? What example does Bogus present? Which do you find more persuasive, and why?

Organizations to Contact

The editors have compiled the following list of organizations concerned with the issues debated in this book. The descriptions are derived from materials provided by the organizations. All have publications or information available for interested readers. The list was compiled on the date of publication of the present volume; names, addresses, and phone numbers, fax numbers, and e-mail addresses may change. Be aware that many organizations take several weeks or longer to respond to inquiries, so allow as much time as possible.

American Alliance for Rights and Responsibilities
1725 K St. NW, Suite 1112
Washington, DC 20006
(202) 785-7844

The alliance believes that the defense of individual rights must be balanced with a commitment to individual and social responsibilities, and hence it works to restore the balance between rights and responsibilities in American society. It publishes the bimonthly newsletter *Re: Rights and Responsibilities.*

American Civil Liberties Union (ACLU)
132 W. 43rd St.
New York, NY 10036
(212) 944-9800

The ACLU is a national organization that works to defend Americans' civil rights guaranteed by the U.S. Constitution. The ACLU publishes and distributes policy statements, pamphlets, and the semiannual newsletter *Civil Liberties Alert.*

American Enterprise Institute
1150 17th St. NW
Washington, DC 20036
(202) 862-5800

This conservative think tank analyzes national and international economic, political, and social issues. It publishes the bimonthly journal the *American Enterprise.*

American Psychiatric Association (APA)
1400 K St. NW
Washington, DC 20005
(202) 682-6000

This professional association promotes psychiatric research and education, helps create mental health policies, and defines professional standards for the field of psychiatry. It publishes the monthly *American Journal of Psychiatry.*

American Psychological Association (APA)
750 First St. NE
Washington, DC 20002-4242
(202) 336-5500

This society of psychologists aims to "advance psychology as a science, as a profession, and as a means of promoting human welfare." It publishes the monthly newspaper *APA Monitor* and the quarterly *Journal of Abnormal Psychology*.

Communitarian Network
2130 H St. NW, Rm. 714J
Washington, DC 20052
(202) 994-4355

The network promotes communitarian policies and a balance of rights and responsibilities. It publishes the quarterly journal the *Responsive Community*.

False Memory Syndrome Foundation
3401 Market St., Suite 130
Philadelphia, PA 19104-3315
(215) 387-1865

The foundation provides counseling and legal aid to victims of False Memory Syndrome (FMS) and their families. According to the foundation, FMS is a condition in which a person's identity has become distorted by an objectively false memory of a traumatic experience. The foundation publishes the booklet *Frequently Asked Questions* and other working papers on FMS.

The Heritage Foundation
214 Massachusetts Ave. NE
Washington, DC 20002-4999
(202) 546-4400

The Heritage Foundation is a conservative public policy research institute that advocates limited government and other conservative values. Its publications include the monthly *Policy Review*, the Backgrounder series of policy papers, and the Heritage Lecture series.

Incest Survivors Resource Network International (ISRNI)
PO Box 7375
Las Cruces, NM 88006-7375
(505) 521-4260

ISRNI is a Quaker educational resource. It promotes awareness of mother-son incest and of the concept of emotional incest. It offers bibliographies and networking information that enables survivors of incest to contact local self-help groups throughout the United States.

Narcotics Anonymous (NA)
World Service Office
PO Box 9999
Van Nuys, CA 91409-9999
(818) 773-9999
fax: (818) 700-0700

Narcotics Anonymous is a twelve-step program that helps drug addicts overcome the disease of addiction. The World Service Office distributes starter kits to addicts forming self-help groups. Its publications include the monthly *NA Way Magazine* and *Meeting by Mail* newsletter as well as numerous brochures.

National Organization for Victim Assistance (NOVA)
1757 Park Rd. NW
Washington, DC 20010
(202) 232-6682

NOVA advocates victims' rights in the criminal justice process and provides educational and technical assistance to justice and counseling professionals who work with victims. It publishes the periodic *Victim Rights and Services: A Legislative Directory* and the annual *Victim Rights Campaign*.

National Victim Center
2111 Wilson Blvd., Suite 300
Arlington, VA 22201
(703) 276-2880

The center is committed to securing rights and fair treatment for victims of violent crime and to reducing violence in American society. It promotes laws to secure rights in the criminal justice process for victims of crime. The center publishes numerous brochures, research papers, and manuals as well as a monthly newsletter, *Networks*.

National Victims Resource Center/National Criminal Justice Reference Service (NCJRS)
PO Box 6000
Rockville, MD 20850
(800) 627-6872

For a fee, the NCJRS will provide topical searches and reading lists on many areas of criminal justice, including victims' rights.

Reason Foundation
3415 S. Sepulveda Blvd., Suite 400
Los Angeles, CA 90034
(310) 391-2245

This public policy organization researches contemporary social and political problems and promotes individualist philosophy and free market principles. It publishes the monthly *Reason* magazine, which has contained numerous articles on the victimhood phenomenon.

Bibliography of Books

Louise Armstrong   *Rocking the Cradle of Sexual Politics: What Happened When Women Said Incest.* Reading, MA: Addison-Wesley, 1994.

Ellen Bass and   *The Courage to Heal: A Guide for Women Survivors of Child Sexual Abuse.* 3rd ed. New York: HarperPerennial, 1994.

William J. Bennett   *The Index of Leading Cultural Indicators: Facts and Figures on the State of American Society.* New York: Simon & Schuster, 1994.

William J. Bennett, ed. *The Book of Virtues: A Treasury of Great Moral Stories.* New York: Simon & Schuster, 1993.

Richard Bernstein   *Dictatorship of Virtue: Multiculturalism and the Battle for America's Future.* New York: Knopf, 1994.

Stephen L. Carter   *The Culture of Disbelief: How American Law and Politics Trivialize Religious Devotion.* New York: BasicBooks, 1993.

Ellis Cose   *A Man's World: How Real Is Male Privilege and How High Is Its Price?* New York: HarperCollins, 1995.

George P. Fletcher   *With Justice for Some: Victims' Rights in Criminal Trials.* Reading, MA: Addison-Wesley, 1995.

John Kenneth Galbraith   *The Culture of Contentment.* Boston: Houghton Mifflin, 1992.

Mary Ann Glendon   *A Nation Under Lawyers: How the Crisis in the Legal Profession Is Transforming American Society.* New York: Farrar, Straus, and Giroux, 1994.

Mary Ann Glendon   *Rights Talk: The Impoverishment of Political Discourse.* New York: Free Press, 1991.

Ellen Goodman   *Value Judgments.* New York: Farrar, Straus, and Giroux, 1993.

Judith Lewis Herman   *Trauma and Recovery.* New York: BasicBooks, 1992.

Gertrude Himmelfarb   *The De-Moralization of Society: From Victorian Virtues to Modern Values.* New York: Knopf, 1995.

Robert Hughes   *Culture of Complaint: The Fraying of America.*
                         New York: Oxford University Press, 1993.

James Davison Hunter   *Before the Shooting Begins: Searching for Democ-*
                         racy in America's Culture War. New York: Free
                         Press, 1994.

Wendy Kaminer   *It's All the Rage: Crime and Culture.* Reading,
                         MA: Addison-Wesley, 1995.

Christopher Lasch   *The Revolt of the Elites: And the Betrayal of Democ-*
                         racy. New York: Norton, 1995.

Michael Lewis   *The Culture of Inequality.* Amherst: University of
                         Massachusetts Press, 1993.

Elizabeth Loftus and   *The Myth of Repressed Memory: False Memories*
Katherine Ketcham   *and Allegations of Sexual Abuse.* New York: St.
                         Martin's Press, 1994.

Myron Magnet   *The Dream and the Nightmare: The Sixties' Legacy*
                         to the Underclass. New York: Morrow, 1993.

John McKnight   *The Careless Society: Community and Its Counter-*
                         feits. New York: BasicBooks, 1995.

Richard John Neuhaus   *America Against Itself: Moral Vision and the Pub-*
                         lic Order. Notre Dame, IN: University of Notre
                         Dame Press, 1992.

Richard Ofshe and   *Making Monsters: False Memories, Psychotherapy,*
Ethan Watters   *and Sexual Hysteria.* New York: Scribner's, 1994.

Walter K. Olson   *The Litigation Explosion: What Happened When*
                         America Unleashed the Lawsuit. New York: Tru-
                         man Talley Books–Dutton, 1991.

Mark Pendergrast   *Victims of Memory: Incest Accusations and Shat-*
                         tered Lives. Hinesburg, VT: Upper Access Books,
                         1995.

Jonathan Rauch   *Kindly Inquisitors: The New Attacks on Free*
                         Thought. Chicago: University of Chicago Press,
                         1993.

Arthur M.   *The Disuniting of America.* New York: Norton,
Schlesinger Jr.   1991.

Richard Stivers   *The Culture of Cynicism: American Morality in*
                         Decline. Cambridge, MA: Blackwell, 1994.

Charles Taylor   *Multiculturalism and "The Politics of Recognition."*
                         Princeton, NJ: Princeton University Press, 1992.

Lenore Terr *Unchained Memories: True Stories of Traumatic Memories, Lost and Found.* New York: Harper-Collins, 1994.

Hollida Wakefield and Ralph Underwager *Return of the Furies: An Investigation into Recovered Memory Therapy.* Chicago: Open Court, 1994.

Claudette Wassil-Grimm *Diagnosis for Disaster: The Devastating Truth About False Memory Syndrome and Its Impact on Accusers and Families.* Woodstock, NY: Overlook Press, 1995.

James Q. Wilson *On Character.* Washington, DC: American Enterprise Institute Press, 1995.

Michael D. Yapko *Suggestions of Abuse: True and False Memories of Childhood Sexual Trauma.* New York: Simon & Schuster, 1994.

Index

CONCLUSION

The conclusion is the part of the book where the author summarizes all that he's said in a profound way.

For weeks I tried to think of a profound conclusion to this book. Something that would crystallize the many groundbreaking points I made throughout it, but I couldn't come up with anything profound.

Unfortunately, I had to conclude that I am not a profound person. This really hurt, and made me feel very, very bad for the thousands of people I have conversed with over the last 51 years.

So I tried to imagine myself as a profound person, so I could imagine what a profound person would say if a profound person were writing a groundbreaking book about T-Ball and Hot Moms n' shit. But as much as I tried to see myself as the generic profound person, I just couldn't come up anything.

Then I thought that it might work if I thought of myself as a specific, real profound person. You know, I would try to think like that dude does and come up with something profound that way. So I imagined I was Morley Safer and imagined what he would say if he were writing a groundbreaking book about T-Ball and Hot Moms n' shit. But I just couldn't imagine what Morley Safer would say about T-Ball and Hot Moms n' shit.

I was at a loss in my quest to draft a meaningful conclusion to my book.

But then it hit me – the conclusion to my book couldn't possibly be profound because it's about T-Ball and Hot Moms n' shit, a subject that could never justify genuine profoundry. So, I logically concluded that even a profoundless person such as me, who is coincidently the author, has the capacity to write the conclusion to this book.

What a relief that was.

MY NOT SO PROFOUND CONCLUSION

My final comments are directed to you Coach Dads out there. Throughout these United States, you're the coaches, assistant coaches, and league officers who run youth sports leagues. It's your show dudes. If you have the right priorities, kids are going to have fond memories of the few years they played organized sports. If you don't, you'll leave many of them with a bad feeling about youth sports that they will keep for the rest of their lives.

So in order to help ya'll – because I'm the kind of guy who likes to help – I'm going to reveal to you the *Jack Malley System for Coaching Youth Sports*. After many years of trial and error, deep thought, analysis, and late night drafting, I was able to piece together my system for the benefit of coaches, kids and families everywhere. It may seem a little complicated at first, but I think you will be able to pick it up. So, without further ado, let me present the *Jack Malley System for Coaching Youth Sports*:

1. It's about the kids, not you;

2. Study your sport so you can actually teach the kids something; and

3. Don't be a win at all costs jerk.

Sincerely,
Jack Malley, Founder
Jack Malley System for Coaching Youth Sports

MEET THE LUNATICS

But wait, you thought the book was (mercifully) over didn't you? Well believe it or not, this book is so damn good that there's even more of it to read after the conclusion, and even after I revealed the true secrets of coaching through the *Jack Malley System for Coaching Youth Sports.*

Following on the very next page, we introduce our brand new comic strip. Move over *Doonesbury,* here comes *Joe Brady, Youth Sports Mogul.*

INTRODUCING JOE BRADY, YOUTH SPORTS MOGUL

He's short, barely 5′ 9″. He's not a smart man, but that does not matter, for he believes he is and will tell you so. Despite his intelligence deficit, he pushes and bumbles forward during every meeting, ball game and discussion, a politically incorrect bull in a politically correct kids sports china shop. Through his unrelenting persistence, he gets the better of his smarter opponents, who are flummoxed by his far too evident ignorance and decline to call him on it out of Yankee modesty.

He often tells the kids and parents of his imagined athletic prowess, his triumphant days of yore, when he was king, an alleged baseball, football and basketball star. When the listeners of these war stories inquire as to the high school at which he performed these miraculous feats, he tells them it was in Pennsylvania, conveniently far from Rolling Hills, Connecticut, the town he now owns.

He does not stray from the weekend wardrobe that has served him so well for many years. During the baseball and football seasons, he goes with a white "Coach" polo shirt, black Adidas sweat pants, a ball cap and cleats. During basketball season, he simply disregards the hat and replaces the cleats with sneakers. When attending social events, he goes with the classic blue blazer and no sock loafer look favored by country clubbers circa 1975. He wears a cheap toupee that fools no one and provides easy material for his detractors.

He is fond of saying that he teaches his players to be winners. Of course, it doesn't hurt that he unfailingly gets the best

players in town on his team by recruiting their fathers to be his assistant coach. He's not much on teaching the nuances of the sports he coaches. Rather, his "coaching" consists primarily of regaling the kids with stories of his amazing sports exploits back in the day; screaming in the faces of his little players when they screw-up; yelling at umpires and referees believing that he can intimidate them because of his "important" status; and dumping as much work as possible on his assistant coaches.

The star of all his teams is the last of his three sons, Chipper. It's no matter that Chipper can barely walk and chew gum at the same time, he is the shortstop, quarterback and point guard of his dad's teams. Any parent who dares to challenge Chipper's ability to play these positions is put down in a manner that would make any mafia Don proud.

While he often tells folks that he takes great pride at being a coach "first," he relishes his power as president of various kids leagues, and wields it in blind ignorance of the rampant political correctness that pervades the kids sports scene. Consistent with this politically incorrect executive style, Joe's teams play to win at all costs, and he gives his players such things as Yodels, Mountain Dew and Red Bull for a team snack.

He is, of course, a lawyer, and president of his country bar where he hobnobs with various local power brokers in a loud back-slapping style. Last but not least, he is married to Kathleen, his wife of twenty years, who idolizes him and waits on him hand and foot, like a slightly smarter, country club version of Edith Bunker. Of course, that doesn't stop him from constantly hitting on hot soccer moms, who revile him and rebuke his blunt advances without fail.

Who is this man? He is Joe Brady, youth sports mogul.

JACK MALLEY

JOE BRADY, THE PHILOSOPHER

JOE BRADY, YOUTH SPORTS MOGUL™

"SO WHAT DOES JOE BRADY BELIEVE IN,
YOU'RE PROBABLY SAYING TO YOURSELF,
WHAT IS JOE BRADY'S PHILOSOPHY?"

LET ME INTRODUCE MYSELF, I'M
JOE BRADY, THE BRAINS BEHIND
PRESCOTT'S PICTURE FRAMING, THE
BEST TEAM IN THE ROLLING HILLS
BASKETBALL LEAGUE.

OH GREAT, JOHN
LENNON ON BASKETBALL,
WHAT A BLOWHARD.

WELL, LET ME TELL YOU HOW
JOE BRADY THINKS, LET ME TELL
YOU THE JOE BRADY CREDO – I DON'T
BELIEVE IN KENNEDY, I DON'T BELIEVE
IN ELVIS, NOR ZIMMERMAN,
I JUST BELIEVE IN JOE BRADY.

UNEQUAL PROTECTION
OF THE LAW

JOE BRADY, YOUTH SPORTS MOGUL™

REFERENCES

AthleticSearch.com, "Problems with Parents? Frank Smoll gives tips on how to handle those parents who cross the line" (August 20, 2012)

HamdenSoccer.com, "The Ten Commandments for Soccer Parents" (August 21, 2012)

AbrahamLincolnOnline.org, Speeches & Writings, Advice to Lawyers "Letter to Isham Reavis on November 5, 1855" (August 21, 2012)

ParentDish.com, "Mayor Steals from Little League" Jennifer Jordan, April 21, 2008 (August 12, 2012)

NCTimes.com, "Ex-President of Vista American Little League Gets Jail for Stealing Funds," Teri Figueroa, May 2, 2007 (August 12, 2012)

ESPN.com, "Baseball Coach Convicted of Two Lesser Counts", September 14, 2006 (August 25, 2012)

Post-Gazette.com, "Jury Convicts T-Ball Coach of Beaning", September 15, 2006 (August 25, 2012)

SI Vault, "Bitter Tee, A Pennsylvania Tee-Ball Coach is Charged with Conspiracy to Injure a Disabled Child", August 8, 2005 (August 25, 2012)

AutismToday.com, "Coach Jailed for Beaning Autistic Player" (August 25, 2012)

SLTrib.com, Monson, "Weighing Compassion, Drive to Win", August 9, 2006 (August 25, 2012)

Reading Eagle, Al McGuire: Profile of Marquette Coach (March 11, 1971)

Newsday.com, "Carneseca Says Jackson is Good Fit for Knicks," Jim Baumbach, May 6, 2008 (August 29, 2012)

ESPN.com, "N.J. Football Coach Arrested for Role in Brawl", October 21, 2006 (August 31, 2012)

Articles.latimes.com, "Antiviolence Leader Goes Anti-antiviolent", November 8, 2001 (August 31, 2012)

HeraldTribune.com, "Sarasota Football Coach Convicted of Battery of Referee", June 20, 2012 (August 31, 2012)